Hand Jive

AMERICAN SIGN LANGUAGE FOR REAL LIFE

Illustrations by Nicole Kaufman
Designed by Stacey May

2006 MetroBooks

ISBN-13: 978-0-7607-7482-3
ISBN-10: 0-7607-7482-X

Printed and bound in China by C&C Offset Printing Co., Inc.

10 9 8 7 6 5 4 3 2 1

DEDICATION

This book is dedicated to Deaf children who, in the past, were required to have their hands bound behind their backs in school so they would use their voices, instead of their hands, to talk. Our book is a celebration of freed hands everywhere.

ACKNOWLEDGMENTS

We wish to thank SuperAgent Matt Wagner of Fresh Books Literary Agency who always tends the good fight; Ruth O'Brien, our Barnes & Noble editor who makes everything better; our illustrator Nicole Kaufman who did a fine job matching the effervescent spirit of ASL; and Nathaniel Marunas of Barnes & Noble who shot us a thumbs up to start this book.

We also express our gratitude to Dr. Howard Stein who taught us why aesthetic and body are never separate and forever equal, and to the late Marshall Jamison, who taught us how good writing shares a truth that—even if crushed to the ground—always rises again.

We are grateful for Jack The Cat—our grumpy and exotic bi-color Persian—who kept the long nights warm and the short days full of purring, even though he'd never want anyone to know.

Janna M. Sweenie

If not for my teacher, Mavis Thies, at the mainstream Hearing school DeForest Elementary in Council Bluffs, Iowa—who failed me in Kindergarten, to encourage my parents to recognize my Deafness and enroll me at the Iowa School for the Deaf—I would not be the well-educated Deaf woman I am today. Mrs. Thies, who was killed three months ago in a car crash, taught me that sometimes beautiful things are born from failure. That is a lesson everyone knows but few are lucky to learn firsthand and, for that gift, I thank her.

I also want to thank all my American Sign Language students over the years who taught me how to teach. Thanks also to my husband, David W. Boles, who was brave to write this book with me and who is talented enough to tempt bringing out the true beauty of ASL as text on the page. Finally, I want to thank my mother, Janet Sweenie, who accepted my Deafness and gave me the best childhood you could hope for and left me wanting for nothing.

David W. Boles

Thank you to my beloved wife, Janna M. Sweenie, for agreeing to share her light with the world in our book. Every day she teaches me the real context of love and language through her immense patience, her brilliant mind, her kind heart, and those beautiful hands.

Contents

Introduction

AMERICA'S THIRD LANGUAGE

Hand Jive: *American Sign Language for Real Life* examines the popular rise of American Sign Language (ASL) and the culture that supports it. We'll demonstrate on each page, with stories and real-life examples, just how ASL exists in the lives of those who love it enough to learn it. By the time you turn the final page, you'll be able to sign like a Deaf person.

Who Are These People?

In the Deaf community, you always introduce yourself and define your connections to other people, so we'll briefly introduce ourselves to you now. We are Janna M. Sweenie and David W. Boles, and we live this book every day. We hope you can learn from the mistakes and successes we share here. Janna, born Deaf in Iowa, attended the Iowa School for the Deaf, and became one of the first Deaf graduates of Lehman College at the City University of New York. Her master's degree in Deafness Rehabilitation is from New York University, and she currently works for the New York State Education Department, helping disabled people find jobs. For more than fifteen years, Janna has taught all levels of American Sign Language at New York University. Her other ASL teaching credits include posts at Montclair State University, CUNY-Lehman, the College of New Rochelle, CUNY-LaGuardia, and Catholic Charities of Brooklyn.

David, a Hearing boy born in Nebraska, has been married to Janna for the past eighteen years, and he writes and teaches on an array of Deaf issues; his master of fine arts degree is from Columbia University in New York City. A former ASL teacher at NYU, David is a private ASL tutor and the public head of curriculum for the Hardcore ASL learning site he and Janna operate at http://HardcoreASL.com. Check out HardcoreASL.com for videos of the signs in this book. Follow the links to the *Hand Jive* videos. At times, we'll pop up in a sidebar or two to share a personal experience from the warp and woof of our lives together to give real-life meaning to the technical stuff we share with you here.

Ancient Signs

Before we jump into American Sign Language, let's drop back a bit into the mists of the past and look at why figuring out how to best talk to each other has been such a hard thing to get a hold of for so long. When we were babies and first discovered there were others in the world and tried to make a connection with someone, we quickly got frustrated at not being understood and by not being able to understand. The history of humankind was shaped by the desire of people to connect with others and to be understood, though real understanding often remains elusive.

Many times, understanding someone new starts with silence: a glance, a handshake, a smile. Silence is golden for a reason: there are fewer opportunities to be misunderstood because mime, body movement, and facial expression all share universal meaning across cultures and countries. A smile in the United States means the same thing in Japan and Russia and New Zealand.

In the ancient world, early forms of communication were recorded on cave walls. Later, Egyptian paintings on tomb walls told stories of daily life to future generations. We think of those picture stories as images in sign. Those old paintings on cave and tomb walls still touch us today because every image tells a story, and you can universally understand the drawn ideas in the same way you can understand the meaning in a smile.

In this book, you'll learn to throw signs in the air instead of painting them onto cave walls. The handshapes and signs you'll see in this book will become imprints as strong and as lasting as the images that still leap out at us today from sooty cave walls.

This Ain't Yo Mama's ASL!

This book is unlike any other American Sign Language book out there because it's raw and raunchy and real. You'll learn the signs and concepts and slang for words like *fuck* and *pussy* and *cock* and *shit*. Don't you dare call this a textbook because it isn't one! In fact, if you're a current student of ASL, some of what we show you here might look unfamiliar and crude because this isn't textbook-perfect ASL. This is real-life ASL, and the street has its own glossing and grammar. We'll do our best to explain exactly what's going on in these concepts so you'll have signposts to follow based on your previous signing experience. If you're new to ASL, that's great—you'll sign these sentences more naturally because we won't have to explain how to tweak what you may have already learned. This is a handbook, a field guide, a set of clues for the way people in the Deaf community speak to each other. This is not pretty-and-perfect ASL. This book will teach you street ASL or slang ASL or, as we say in the title, *Hand Jive!*

Code of the Smoke

Let's understand how people have improved their ability to connect with each other over time and space. We mentioned drawings on cave walls as a way in which a generation has spoken to future generations; another form of images as signs is smoke signals. Native American tribes could communicate silently with each other over vast distances by lighting fires and using blankets to smother the flames a bit to create smoke that they would release into the air in specific and predetermined intervals to be read by faraway others who knew the secret code of the smoke. Smoke signals were a form of silent Morse code and also a type of signed language in billows of ash.

Code-Switching

The key to decoding signals in both smoke and American Sign Language is understanding the cultural codes of the people who use the language and then switching between those codes as you cross cultures. "Code-switching" is knowing that in the Hearing world, calling someone fat is an insult, while in Deaf culture, calling someone fat may hurt a bit but it is ordinary and expected. Communication signals can quickly get crossed if someone misses a code-switch. This book will help you meander across gaps in cultural understanding and ease you into the world of the Deaf, so you can code-switch at will without fear of insulting someone or feeling insulted. We will discuss how to do this in Chapter 1.

Sign of the Signs

There are other forms of signed language you may have seen in addition to the language of the Deaf. Many Plains tribes, like the Ojibwa, Lakota, Kiowa, Cheyenne, and Arapaho, used signed language to communicate with their home tribe and with other tribes. Signed language and universal gestures were used by Native Americans to create a common base of understanding among the variety of dialects and accents of spoken Native American languages: hands raised high in the air meant "peace" across all Native American cultures just as, in the "white man's world," an extended palm for shaking meant "peace"—because an open hand cannot grasp a weapon.

You may have seen "gang signs" on television or on the street. Those signs are also inspired by sign language, though they have a completely different meaning and intent than ASL. Gang signs are indicative of a closed culture. You know what the signs mean only because you've been accepted and trained in the ways of that culture. Those signs become tethers to others like you, and together you create new vocabulary and meaning based on your group's particular context—just like ASL. The difference between gang signs and ASL is that gang signs rely mainly on "home" signs to be understood.

"Home" signs are made-up signs that a few people agree to use by applying meaning to the concept in question. Many young Deaf children use home signs with their Hearing family members as a way to communicate without having to formally learn ASL. Instead of using the ASL sign for milk, a home-signing child might just clench his fists together in a certain way. No one else would know that "clenching fists" means "milk," but outsiders don't need to understand for the sign to have its effect. Only those in the family core need to learn, understand, and agree upon the sign's meaning. Even ASL has home signs—they are usually regional or school-based.

HISTORY

The Animal Children

To really understand why ASL is so important in the education and job opportunities afforded the Deaf, we need to examine some history of how the Deaf were viewed and treated. Typically, those outside the Deaf culture, and especially those in the medical community, have always seen the Deaf as "broken" and needing to have their ears fixed by surgery and technology. Many people born Deaf do not see themselves as broken, and they identify and relate to the world on a visual plane. That historically did not sit well with those in charge of "fixing" Deaf people, and the sight of young Deaf children "clawing the air" and using "Deaf voicing" was not looked upon kindly by society, because it made the children look and sound guttural and feral and it was a bad influence on the good Hearing children of the land. So the Deaf children were shuttered away in institutions where they would invent home signs to talk to each other.

You Are a Deaf Infant

Now imagine you are a Deaf baby born to Hearing parents and what it must be like to be fed information and to experience interaction only through mainly one sense: your sight. You don't hear your parents chatting nearby. You don't hear the traffic outside. You don't hear the television or the radio or your mother's favorite music. You just lie in your bassinet, flat on your back, looking up at your mobile swaying in the breeze. You yearn for a face to pop in over you for interaction. Unfortunately, all you can do then is stare at the face and try to read its features. You can't hear what is being said to you. Your parents don't know that ASL is your language. Your universe is different from theirs, though you all share space in the world in the same home.

Will your parents accept your Deafness and learn American Sign Language, even though from the moment you're born you're already developmentally behind other babies who can hear? Or will your parents opt to listen to the medical community and try to "fix" you with a cochlear implant? The chances are greater than 95 percent that your Hearing parents will take the medical route to fix you, because there is comfort in technology and the medical profession, and there's always the hope that you be will more like them one day as you try, for the rest of your life, to pass in the mainstream as Hearing. In olden days, your hands would have been bound behind your back in school to prevent you from using them to communicate. Your voice, some educators reckoned, was your only viable means of communication, even though few could understand the Deaf sounds you were forced to utter.

Language as Civilization

Language civilizes people and tames nations. Like morality and law alike, a common language shares promises and ideas that many people can understand and hold dear. The American Deaf were in need of a formal, sustained, and teachable language, and Thomas Hopkins Gallaudet came to the rescue.

Hope in a Hat

In the 1800s in the United States, Thomas Hopkins Gallaudet noticed a girl named Alice Cogswell being ignored by her peers. When he investigated, he discovered she was Deaf. In an attempt to communicate with her, he took off his hat, pointed to it, and then scratched out H-A-T in a gravel driveway. Alice was able to make the connection between the abstract letters of the word and the object, and Gallaudet decided he wanted to teach her on a consistent basis.

Gallaudet knew he had to find a language to teach Alice, so he traveled to Europe and found Laurent Clerc—a Deaf man and a Deaf educator—at the Paris School for the Deaf to help him.

Enter that French Guy

On the trip back to the United States, Clerc and Gallaudet taught each other their respective languages: Clerc taught Gallaudet French sign language; Gallaudet taught Clerc English. Together they invented a new language for the Deaf, called American Sign Language. Since there's a strong French base in American Sign Language, those who know a bit of French before they begin their ASL studies do extremely well, as they can more quickly connect the commonly shared conceits because ASL grammar is similar to French.

In 1817, Clerc and Gallaudet created the American School for the Deaf, in Hartford, Connecticut, and Laurent Clerc became the first Deaf educator in a Deaf school in America. Forty years later, Gallaudet's son Edward would move to Washington, D.C., to run a school for the Deaf. In 1864, President Abraham Lincoln signed a charter for Gallaudet University, named in honor of Edward's father, which became the first national Deaf college in America.

The Lincoln Legend

Folklore has it that the Lincoln Memorial in Washington, D.C., bears a secret tribute to the Deaf and the work of President Lincoln in helping set up Gallaudet University's charter. Look at the way in which Lincoln's left hand is sculpted; many claim it is positioned in the manual alphabet handshape letter *A* and that Lincoln's right hand is sculpted in a relaxed *L* handshape, thus creating, from Lincoln's point of view anyway, his initials, "A. L." That story has been both supported and debunked, but every Deaf person we know instantly recognizes the "A. L." handshapes before learning of the folklore. This story may be more than a myth, because the artist who sculpted the Lincoln Memorial statue, Daniel Chester French, also created, twenty-six years earlier, the statue of Thomas Hopkins Gallaudet and Alice Cogswell that sits on the university campus. Gallaudet, in that statue, is teaching Alice the handshape for... *A*.

Birth of a Notion

Gallaudet and Clerc's success in inventing American Sign Language led to a more calculated and sustained vision for the schooling of Deaf children across America. Many states created their own Deaf institutions where Deaf children were taught ASL. There are many different forms of communication for the Deaf today, and not all signed language you see is necessarily ASL.

SIGNED LANGUAGE

ASL as a Foreign Language

You might think, with ASL's deep roots in French, that ASL would be readily accepted as a foreign language credit for university study. Not so fast! While many major universities now accept American Sign Language as a foreign language, many colleges still think that ASL is just signed English. Janna argued to have ASL fulfill her foreign language credit in college—you'll read about that story in Chapter 1. There are lots of studies and scholarly information that will back up your claim that ASL is not, in any way, English. Now we'll introduce some of the various forms of sign language you might see being used.

SEE

SEE means "Signing Exact English," and this is used by those who wish to teach Deaf students precise English grammar and sentence structure. Word endings like -*ing* are added to signs—usually via finger spelling—in order to "English-ize" them. Some Hearing educators feel SEE is the best way to teach the Deaf because exactly what is being voiced matches exactly what is being signed. We feel SEE can be confusing because ASL is not SEE and to use ASL structure with SEE word endings makes learning harder than it should be for Deaf students.

Cued Speech

Cued speech uses a series of eight handshapes that are placed around the mouth and face to give a Deaf child hints on how spoken words differ in sound. Cued speech, while interesting, isn't tremendously popular in Deaf education because it relies heavily on voice and lipreading. While lipreading can be learned, few Deaf ever become expert at it because, like a fingerprint, everyone's lips are unique and each set of lips pronounces the same words differently.

Rochester Method

The Rochester Method is fascinating to watch. It is not a signed language—the Rochester Method is 100 percent finger spelling! Every single word that is being spoken is finger spelled, with nary a pause between words. It's beautiful to watch but a little difficult to understand and perform if you don't have a lot of experience and patience. Interpreters who use the Rochester Method quickly get tired fingers!

PSE

PSE stands for "Pidgin Signed English." This is the most common form of signed language you see in America today, and we feel it is a bastardization of American Sign Language and English. A "pidgin" is a simplified speech invented to foster communication between people who use different languages. So PSE is a rickety bridge between the Deaf and the Hearing world, and misunderstanding and mis-communication happen a lot. In interpreting sessions, you'll usually see PSE used if voice is part of the translation. You don't use voiced word pronunciation in ASL, but if you're interpreting between a Deaf person and a Hearing person, the inter-preter will likely use PSE with voice to try to cover all the bases. Many American Sign Language programs that claim to teach ASL actually teach only PSE. It is common for students to take our classes and immediately get lost if they have previous sign language experience, because they were taught PSE and not ASL.

Total Communication

Total communication is another bridging concept. "Total communication" means using any mixture of ASL or PSE or SEE with voicing to cover as many conceptual bases as possible. Total communication strives to have it all, but we feel it lacks a consistent core of established understanding.

ABOUT HAND JIVE

The style of ASL that we teach is "hardcore," and that's what you'll find in this book. Hardcore ASL is ASL signed in the way in which those in the Deaf community use it in their lives. We don't fret about textbook-perfect sentence construction or precise translations from English to ASL. We're more concerned about expressing concepts and ideas. Sometimes to get those points across you need to do more than just follow the established rules of Gallaudet and Clerc. Languages evolve over generations. This hardcore ASL we'll teach you is sort of a Deaf street-slang language with an attitude and a fierceness you won't find in an ordinary ASL classroom. The Deaf community has developed as potent and colorful a vernacular as Hearing folks have, and *Hand Jive* will give you a unique insight into that world. The terms and phrases used in this book are not only fun and interesting, but useful. When we begin to guide you through some sentences and concepts, we'll do it in the same way in which we work with our American Sign Language students in real life. We will be repetitive and really specific in our instructions, and we'll ask you to follow our directions carefully. If you flow with us, you'll discover how the madness in our method works.

The ASL you'll find in this book is the tough stuff that celebrates the hard-won efforts of the Deaf community to establish an identity and to defend a culture against those who believe they know better than those born into a visual, not audible, world.

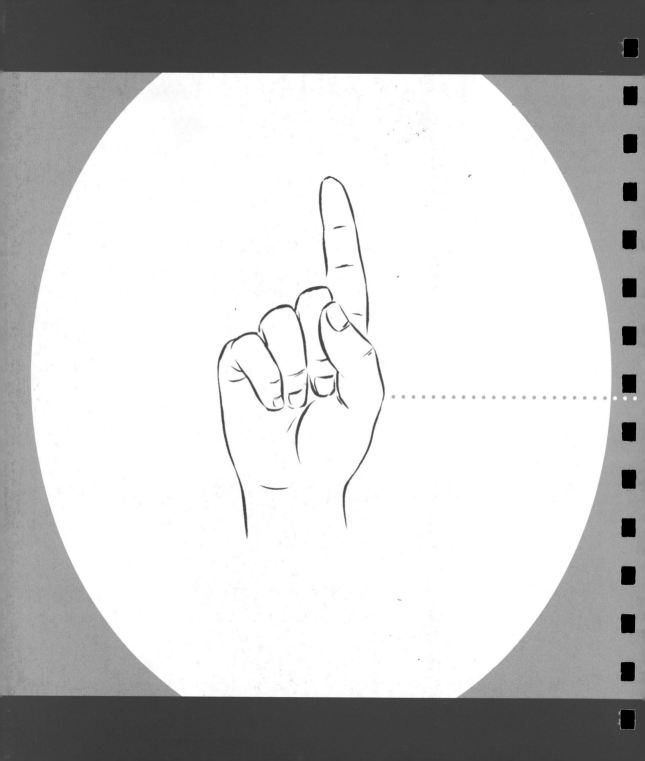

Part One

DEAF CULTURE

1 Getting Down with the Deaf

Now that you have a brief background on how the Deaf came to use American Sign Language to talk to each other, let's take a look at all the people who use American Sign Language. This chapter will examine the Deaf—their culture, their norms—and those who love them. A "Deaf norm" means the Deaf way or the Deaf custom of doing things. Here are our "sweet sixteen" Deaf norms.

Deaf Norm #1: ASL is the Most Important Deaf Norm

ASL is a Deaf norm and a Deaf norm is ASL, so you can't separate the two, though people have tried. The Deaf world is defined by ASL, and when you go to Deaf events you can witness the beauty of sign. If you go to a football game at Gallaudet, you'll see a wave of arms and hands, sometimes signing in unison, as a big bass drum pounds out the snap count for the Deaf players on the field. ASL is not English. They do not share the same grammar or syntax, as you'll see in Chapter 2 in the "wh-question" section, where you'll see that *what* is not at the start of an ASL sentence. The *what* in a question is at the end of an ASL sentence. If you asked in English "What is your name?" the ASL translation is "you + name + what?"

Deaf Norm #2: Face as a Fountain

Hands aren't the only important things in ASL and Deaf culture. For the Deaf, the face is a fountain of information that quenches your every thirst for content and meaning. Facial expression is vital, as you'll find out in Chapter 2, to understanding precisely what the ASL hands are saying in context. Hearing people know when someone is mad or glad without looking at the person because the tone and volume of the voice give clues to the person's emotional state. Deaf people determine tone and volume by looking at the facial expression of the speaker. Facial expressions not only tell emotion, but in ASL, your facial expression also acts, grammatically speaking, as a verb!

Ten years ago most of our Asian foreign exchange students had a hard time with facial expression in ASL because in their home culture faces were to remain neutral, not animated, while speaking. In the last few years or so, however, Asian students have soared to the top of our classes in their ability to expressively use their faces in communication. Is this the Americanization of a student from a foreign culture, or is this simply a growing pattern in cultures outside the United States to use the face more openly to express emotion?

Deaf President Now

On March 6, 1988, history was made in the Deaf community: a revolt started on the campus of Gallaudet University. We were living in Washington, D.C., at the time, and with the rest of the Gallaudet community of supporters, we marched on Washington and took over the Capitol steps. Gallaudet's trustees had just chosen as the seventh president of the university a person who had no experience in Deaf education and who did not know sign, despite more than one hundred Deaf people with Ph.D.s and experience in administration having also applied for the job. Two of the three finalists for the position were Deaf. The outrage from students and the Deaf community was so strong that Gallaudet was shut down. Members of the board were burned in effigy all across the campus. The Deaf had had enough of the social paternalism that saw them as broken and helpless instead of equal and able.

The students and their supporters won when Dr. I. King Jordan, one of the original Deaf finalists and a longtime faculty member, was named the eighth president of Gallaudet University. Many Hearing people did not understand the importance of the Gallaudet protest or its social significance in the Deaf community, and there were legislators who threatened to withdraw federal funding from Gallaudet if the Deaf wanted to be truly "on their own."

The Deaf President Now protest planted the seeds that would later blossom into law as the Americans with Disabilities Act, signed by the first President Bush on July 26, 1992. The ADA "prohibits private employers, state and local governments, employment agencies and labor unions from discriminating against qualified individuals with disabilities in job application procedures, hiring, firing, advancement, compensation, job training and other terms...." The only job a Deaf person can't legally have currently is that of an airplane pilot, because a pilot must be able to use a headset to communicate with airport towers in an emergency.

Don't Overblow!

One time when Janna was in a meeting, her interpreter, who was pretty good at signing, insisted on blowing air—that's an ASL facial expression that is used only in really specific cases. Usually "blowing air" means "far away" or "way over there," and Janna knew every sentence wasn't about something being far away. As an ASL teacher, Janna sat in the meeting wondering where that interpreter had learned the blowing air style of interpreting. After the meeting, Janna approached the interpreter and explained to him what blowing air really meant, and the interpreter took the feedback pretty well. Sometimes interpreters think they know more than the Deaf they are interpreting for, and the Deaf need to be assertive in offering corrections. Unfortunately, that rarely happens, because the relationship between Deaf and interpreter is one of great power—like the story of how, in the land of the Blind, the one-eyed man is King—and sometimes interpreters see themselves as the source of information and expertise instead of being a transparent conduit between source and receiver. Interpreters are important. The Deaf need them and they need the Deaf. You'll blow air with us in Chapter 2.

Deaf Norm #3:
Hugging Hello, Good-Bye, and Everything In Between

If you plan to spend any time with a Deaf person or attend a Deaf event, prepare to be hugged within an inch of your life! The Deaf love to hug "hello," and hug "I'm so happy for you," and hug "good-bye," and they love to find any other reason to touch in a loving and supportive way. This obsession with hugging can sometimes make Hearing people uncomfortable, but in the Deaf community, touching, tapping on the shoulder, hugging, and waving are all nonintimate, ordinary, everyday forms of physical communication.

Deaf Norm #4: I'm Going to the Bathroom Now!

The Deaf also always announce to everyone in a group precisely what they plan to do if they leave the room or take leave of the group. If you're going home, you announce that you're going home. If you're leaving to visit Mary down the hall, you tell the group exactly what you're doing and when you'll return. Announcing your intent to the group you're with is important to being accepted as a member of the Deaf community.

Deaf Norm #5: How Do You Connect to Me?

Another important connection is to go through the history of who you know and who I know for everyone in the room so you can fit one another in the strata of your lives. We demonstrated how this works when we met you in the Introduction. This can seem tedious and mind-bending to those who aren't familiar with this cultural style of introduction, but, for the Deaf, it is important to know about your friends, family, where you work, and what school you attended. If you're new to ASL and you don't have many friends or experiences in Deaf culture, you can say you're a newbie in ASL, tell the group why you're there to learn, and ask them to help you.

Deaf Norm #6: Gossipy Groups

Sharing who you are and what you've done is just the preamble to the real reason for sharing all those intimate details of your life: gossip! Talking about other people—even with them standing right next to you—is, unfortunately, a common occurrence in the Deaf community, but hey, keep your mouth shut or make something up if you don't want your life spread all around the Deaf universe in a matter of seconds. Pagers and text messaging have taken gossip to an all-new high in the Deaf community. For many Deaf there is no such thing as a secret. Everything must be told. Information, positive or negative (though negative is much more fun to share), belongs to everyone, and gossip becomes rumor becomes legend and some people never recover from the stories told about them because, as you know, not all gossip is true!

This kind of recklessness when it comes to privacy can cause some heated battles in Deaf groups, and knowing what to share with what person can lead you to higher ground. That is a difficult trail to traverse, however, because the "Deaf way" is to be open and to share and chat, but if you're too open or if you share too much, it will come back and bite you hard later. Sometimes, when you are pressed for information that you refuse to give up but that others will not stop asking about, signing "Bite me!" can be an effective rejoinder, which leads us perfectly into our next norm....

Deaf Norm #7: A Blunt You Don't Smoke

"You're fat, you smell, and I hate you!" That blunt sentence can be a common greeting in the Deaf community but it doesn't necessarily mean that someone is being rude to you—it is more like expressing "What happened to you?" in a less formal manner, and the thought behind the statement could be "Are you stressed at work?" or "Did you have an awful breakup?" or "Tell me what happened that

Not So Great on the Skinny

Janna decided to go on a diet to lose some weight and feel healthy. When some people in the Deaf community saw her after she had lost weight they decided, without asking her, that the reason for the rapid weight loss was because she had cancer. The word that Janna had cancer spread all across the Deaf community in New York and she received cards and condolence calls and flowers. It was years before Janna was able to finally put that false gossip to rest. She did not have cancer. She had never had cancer. Janna was just skinnier and healthier.

caused you to get fat!" At times, these blunt questions can hurt feelings and seem insensitive, even to other Deaf people. If you're insulted by these questions, you can just say, "You've gone too far," and the Deaf may listen or they may decide to school you in the ways of the Deaf by getting even more blunt with you.

In the Deaf community, being "brutally blunt" is an accepted way of life. If someone has gained weight, you don't hesitate one moment to make the "fatso" sign the instant you see them. If a woman or man has big breasts, you imitate their jiggly breasts' movement when you see them or mention them to someone else. If someone is behaving in a stupid manner, you do not hesitate for an instant to call them stupid or dumb or idiotic because that's the way of the Deaf. Is there a difference between being blunt and being cruel? It all depends on which end you get, but even the blunt end cuts.

Deaf Norm #8: What's in a Sign Name?

Being blunt can also influence your sign name, because your most obvious physical asset or defect becomes your sign name. That may sound unfair or mean, but the purpose of a sign name is to instantly describe a person so there is no doubt about who's being discussed. Since the Deaf share a visual culture, what you look like is how you're best remembered.

Sometimes these blunt descriptions of people are based on cultural and ethnic stereotypes, and that may not be politically correct. We carefully try to make the case that it's okay to describe a person by how they physically look—even if it may play into a cultural or ethnic stereotype—because in ASL and the Deaf community, accuracy is more important than political correctness or saying the falsely "right" thing that manners and society demand. An example is describing Caucasian people as white-faced because the sign in ASL for "Caucasian" is color-white + back-on-face. While that may play into a stereotype, it's correct in the word definition of "Caucasian," and a particularly "white-faced" person might be assigned a sign name that has to do with being "ghostly" or "bright-skinned" or "one who easily blushes," and that would be accepted in the Deaf community as an appropriate sign name and not as being stereotypical of the Caucasian race.

All this talk about being blunt gives us a deeper understanding of the value and importance of sign names in the Deaf community and, in turn, ASL. Let's examine some sign names and how they came to be used in real-life ASL.

Sign names in the Deaf community are cherished in the same manner in which Native American names are provided in that community. Some might say that mandatory sign names in the Deaf community are kind of like the nicknames mafia members give to each other based on behavior or physical attributes, like "Tommy Two Chins" or "Jimmy Smokes" or "Billy Four Fingers." Not everyone "deserves" a sign name. You earn a sign name from a Deaf person by being actively involved in the Deaf community for a long time. If you aren't in the community, you don't need a sign name to identify you.

Janna's sign name is "J. S.": it's created by touching the opposite shoulder (the letter *J*) and then moving the hand outward to form the letter *S*. We admit it's a boring sign name; it's nondescriptive and sort of English-y, because it uses finger spelling. Finger spelling is more Rochester Method than pure ASL. Deaf people usually give signs based on appearance, so a better sign name for Janna would be "cut on eyebrow," because when she was little, she fell off a swing and the edge of the swing fell back into her and sliced her eyebrow in two—a scar still bisects her right eyebrow today. You would sign Janna's new sign name by taking your right index finger and making a quick "cut" across your right eyebrow. Name signs can change over time as people change, and a Deaf person can invent a new sign name. The question is, will the Deaf community accept the new sign name or will they continue to use your original sign name? Janna stayed with her original "J. S." sign name because that's how people know her and changing now would lead to more confusion than clarity.

Name Ye Not Yourself!

If you are Hearing, your sign name MUST be given to you by a Deaf person. Hearing people cannot create their own sign name, though many try. It's so funny to meet a Hearing person who claims their sign name was given to them by a Deaf person when there's no way in the world that a Deaf person would ever invent that kind of a silly sign. Here's an example: David was once given a sign name by a Hearing actor who was in a play with Janna. Since David is a writer, the actor invented David's sign name using the *D* manual alphabet handshape with one hand and then wiggling the *D* across the palm of his other hand as if he were writing. A sign like that is not ASL and is not an appropriate element of Deaf culture. We can't think of a single legitimate ASL sign name given by a Deaf person that has any kind of interaction with a flat palm.

Janna quickly replaced David's phony sign name with one of her own. The first thing that attracted her to him were his gorgeous hazel eyes because they were—and still are—piercing! Janna created a new name using the sign for "shining" coming out of one eye, so David's new sign name has no manual alphabet handshape—it is, instead, a purely ASL handshape "25" that in English roughly translates to "eyes + shine + coming-out." When Janna introduces David and demonstrates his sign name, the Deaf usually stop for a moment and look at David's eyes to determine the validity of the sign. No one has disagreed yet.

Sometimes you don't like the sign name given to you, and while you can ask that it be changed, there's no guarantee that request will be honored, because often your sign name memorializes your most memorable feature—whether it's shining eyes or a scar through your eyebrow.

Other examples of sign names might be "mole on face" for someone who has an interesting mole that makes them unique, or "cut-off arm" for someone who lost an arm in a war or in a printing-press accident. "Big nose" can be common. Yankees catcher Jorge Posada's ASL sign name is "big ears" because his ears are his most obvious feature, and Yankee Derek Jeter's sign name is "chubby cheeks" because that's his most distinguishing facial feature.

When Janna gives a sign name to a Hearing person, she stays away from English meanings and tries to capture the physical essence of a person. Sign names are usually formed on the chin, forehead, nose, mouth, center of chest, part of an arm, or out away from the chest, and the sign usually moves from the head to the top of the torso. Not everyone has a sign name. If your name is short like "Ed" or "Bill," it's easy to spell "E-D" or "B-I-Double L." Sometimes you have a unique English alphabet handshape that uses the same movement and location to describe different people. Let's say Mary, Janelle, Bonnie, and Dolly all have long, pretty hair. You would probably see the first manual alphabet letter of their names—M, J, B, or D—formed at the top of the head, and then that alphabet shape would elegantly flow down to the shoulder. So the ASL movement for "pretty, flowing hair" can define many people based on a unique handshape. In New York, we know at least twenty people with the same sign name based on hair and we know five people with similar "J on shoulder" sign names. That can be confusing, so if there's any doubt about which person you are referring to, you can move to an even more intimate physical description to better define the "J" or "pretty hair" you want to discuss. If you're confused about who's being discussed, you may interrupt the conversation and ask for clarification. That's common in the Deaf community.

Deaf Norm #9: Don't Read My Lips

ASL does not use a Hearing voice, but ASL is not silent! Sometimes there's the sound of blowing air or a grunt or guttural sound to add to the expression being signed. We call that Deaf speech, but it isn't a Deaf person trying to speak English words. Deaf speech consists mainly of piecemeal staccato pronunciations of parts of English words that belong to ASL sentence structure and give a clue to which synonym is being signed. In ASL, the same sign can mean many things, so Deaf speech plus facial expression gives you the meaning of the same sign in multiple contexts. Sometimes "Ahhhh!" is used to emphasize a point. Be complimented if a Deaf person uses Deaf speech with you, because it means that person is comfortable enough with you to expose a, perhaps, difficult voice to understand without sign. Just remember, not all Deaf use their voice. Some use voice a little. Some never use voice. Some you can't shut up!

After the Gallaudet Deaf President Now revolution, there were buttons created to celebrate the successful appointment of the first Deaf president of the

Lip Reading for Profit

Did you know that some of the best lip-readers are not Deaf people, but Hearing people? It makes sense, since Hearing people hear words and watch mouths as others are speaking and would be able to blend those talents easily in reading silent lips speaking English. Not all Hearing people are good lip-readers, but many fail to measure and exploit this unexplored talent.

Lipreading is a forced talent many Deaf are taught growing up in order to survive in a Hearing world. They work on recognizing lip shapes, which is hard to master. To find a common ground for pronunciation, with regional and international accents tossed into the mix, is a hefty challenge.

Have you ever wondered why baseball players hide their mouths with their gloves when they approach the pitcher's mound or why football coaches hide their mouths behind their playbooks? They are defending against the other team reading their lips and stealing their plans!

university. The buttons had a cartoon drawing of a person with both index fingers poised in the Hearing "We're Number One" shape at each corner of the mouth. Then, the arms and hands—still in that index-finger handshape of triumph—appeared to move out sharply away from the face. The caption on the button said "Pah!" for the character's open-mouthed expression of joy. In the context of Deaf culture and Deaf speech, that "Pah!" simply meant "Finally!"

If you use English lip pronunciations, you're not seeing ASL, you are seeing, as we discussed in the Introduction, Pidgin Signed English. It is not possible to use English voice and ASL at the same time. Expert signers might be able to pull that off for a single sentence or for a brief question, but it can't be done in an extended conversation.

Deaf Norm #10: You Voice, You Die!

It is not appropriate to use your voice but not sign in the Deaf community. If you are at a Deaf event, or if you're in the home of Deaf friends, you need to be able to follow the Deaf norm without feeling you are being forced into behavior that doesn't fit you. If you're new to the Deaf community and don't know many signs, that's okay! Just let the Deaf know you're new to sign language and they'll try to help you communicate. Many Deaf enjoy interacting with the Hearing and they have more ability to code-switch than you do, so once you identify yourself as Hearing they'll leap into action to help you feel welcome. There are always exceptions, so be prepared for the "If you don't know ASL, why are you trying to talk me?" crowd. Just shrug off that attitude and find someone else who's interested in communicating with you. Take a paper and pen with you if you decide to brave a Deaf community event on your own—they'll come in handy.

If a Deaf person decides to use their voice with you, that gives you, in turn, permission to use your voice with them. If there's still a failure to communicate, you may need to write to each other. Writing is always the safest plan. Look at the Deaf person for guidance on how best to proceed, even if it means you have to repeat yourself a few times. If you know a few signs, like "Where is the bathroom?" or "My name is Tom," use them! It doesn't matter if you sign perfectly or not; it's the effort that matters. Sure, some may laugh at you, but laugh along with them, because nobody's perfect and if you knew all the signs, you'd be a paid interpreter instead of a new friend. Most of the Deaf love it when the Hearing are willing to learn the culture of their language, and the more people who speak ASL, the longer it will live as a language.

You might see some really fast signing you cannot follow and you will feel lost. That's okay. Ask them to slow down and to repeat for you as often as you need. Your feeling lost and overwhelmed is a taste of how many Deaf feel in the Hearing world. The easy part is you can get up and leave any time you like to return to your Hearing world with Hearing norms. The Deaf have no way to avoid the Hearing world because the universe revolves around voiced speech and ears that hear, and not all people in the Hearing world want to be bothered with repeating or writing something down because that takes kindness and interest and time, and unfortunately those values are eroding. It is a big relief for the Deaf when they stumble upon a Hearing person willing to help them on their terms.

Deaf Norm #11: Eyes For For?

If you're a seasoned ASL speaker and you happen to be at a Deaf event with a Hearing friend who doesn't sign, you shouldn't use your voice for the benefit of your friend during the event. You, as a fluent signer, should sign ASL at all times. If you need some privacy with your Hearing friend, excuse yourself from the Deaf group and find a private place to speak where no one can see you. For private Deaf-on-Deaf conversations, the Deaf excuse themselves and move to a place where they cannot be seen in order to have a private conversation.

How to Handle an Interpreter

The best interpreters are those who are transparent. They don't try to control or dictate the conversation. They do not invent pieces of conversations or try to explain what is being said. They simply interpret the sentences and ideas as expressed, and if clarification is needed, the person who is confused will ask the other person, not the interpreter, to explain. Interpreters are bound by a code of ethics not to gossip or reveal the conversations they interpret. If you use an interpreter, speak directly to the person you are addressing without looking at, or acknowledging, the interpreter. You can always thank the interpreter after the job is over.

Remember, ASL is a visual language and it's easy to "overeye" conversations. "Overeye" is what we call the Deaf way of overhearing conversations. Signs, unlike voice, can be seen from far away. Don't assume your signing isn't being watched by all the Deaf in the room, and don't assume just because someone is Deaf that they are fluent in ASL. A Deaf person can be illiterate in not only English but in ASL as well. Some Deaf are not born in America, and they have to learn ASL from scratch when they arrive here.

There is no such thing as a private conversation in the Deaf community if you're signing within eyesight. Here's what a friend of ours is fond of saying when the issue of watching ASL conversations that do not concern her comes up: "Eyes for for?" Loosely translated into English that means, "Eyes are for watching, and if I can see your conversation, I will watch it." Get used to being stared at while you are in the Deaf community. Every move you make is being noted and memorized, and for the uninitiated, it can be a little creepy at first. Just stare back. They won't stop staring, but at least you'll feel more like a part of the group!

Deaf Norm #12: Grabbing Attention

There are a lot of ways to grab the attention of a Deaf person, and the Deaf use these methods every day with each other, so you should be prepared to use them with the Deaf and have them used against you, too.

Tapping is a skill, and it takes a master's touch. You touch to get attention by making two quick taps, but not too hard, on the top of the shoulder. You can also tap on the arm, but never on the head or leg if the person is standing up. If the person is seated, you can tap on the lower thigh. You tap when you are within easy reach of the person and you tap because the person is preoccupied in another conversation or looking elsewhere and you want their attention. We used to live in a mainly Deaf apartment building, Tanya Towers, in New York City's Alphabet City neighborhood, and there was a Hearing janitor who was a huge mass of muscle and bone. He would always mop the floors backward, so if you wanted to pass him or let him know you were there so he wouldn't mop into you, you had to tap him on the shoulder because he always had headphones on. Every time we would tap him on the shoulder, in the Deaf way, this hulk of a man would scream in terror. He was not used to being touched. Tapping scared him. If you plan to spend any time in the Deaf community, be prepared to tap, and to be tapped, and try not to scream!

Never wave your hand in front of a Deaf person's face. Not only is it annoying and poor manners, it is also insulting because it's as if you're testing to see if they're Blind as well. Waving is an acceptable form of getting the attention of a Deaf person only when used from a distance. If the Deaf person is within your line of sight and their back is not turned to you, make a big, exaggerated, arcing wave in the hope that you will catch their eye. Hearing people are not good at catching someone waving at them like that, but the Deaf are good at seeing the wave because it is part of their culture. If waving doesn't work, walk over and give a couple of shoulder taps.

You can also stomp your feet to get the attention of the Deaf. That sort of behavior may not be tolerated in the Hearing world, but in Deaf society, stomping is normal and accepted. Wooden floors are best because they make a deep sound that vibrates across the room. You're not jumping up and down, you're just stomping one foot a couple of times. What usually happens in a crowded room is someone else will "catch" your stomp—ask you what you want—and they'll wave or tap or even stomp to continue the communication chain on to the person you want to reach. Stomping is not recommended on a floor with thick carpeting, and if you stomp too much on a concrete floor you might hurt your knee, so just taking a walk over to the person is probably the safest way to grab their attention in that case.

The Deaf are sensitive to lights that flash. The Deaf hear with their eyes, and, when driving, they're more aware of emergency vehicles than their Hearing peers because the Hearing rely mainly on their ears to process external warnings. With practically soundproofed cars, cellular phones, and deluxe surround-sound, hearing ears are kept entertained while driving. The Deaf while driving are always on the lookout for visual clues to tell them what is happening outside their car. If you're in a room full of Deaf people and you want to instantly get their attention, flash the overhead lights a few times.

There's nothing wrong with using your voice to call a Deaf person's name— the Deaf do it all the time—but you need to have the Deaf person's permission before you try it the first time. Some Deaf are sensitive to feeling the voiced vibration of their name, while others are not. When you become friends with a Deaf person and you find yourself in a situation where you cannot stomp, touch, or flash the lights and you forgot to ask permission first to call out their name, trying using a loud voiced sound like "oh!" or "ah!" or "woo!" to get the Deaf person's attention. The Deaf use that kind of inflected voicing to get the attention of other Deaf people. Ask your friend what kind of attention-getting method works best. You'll find out much more about stylized voicing in Chapter 6.

Janna Gets Flashed at Whole Foods

There's a brand-new Whole Foods grocery store at Union Square in Manhattan. The store has twenty cashier lines and workers who direct you to which line to join. The place is always loud and packed with people. Janna usually looks at the cashier's flashing number light to know where she needs to go, since she cannot hear the yelled instruction of the worker at the front of the line who tells you which cashier is available. To Janna's dismay one day, three cashier lights were flashing all at the same time and she didn't know which one to attend. She looked at the worker at the front of the line, caught his attention, and pointed to her ears and shook her head, giving him the universal gesture that she was Deaf.

The guy's eyes widened, but not in a bad way, and Janna thought he was going to yell the number of the line to join. He did not. He came to her and guided her to a cashier and said something to the cashier that Janna did not catch. The cashier gave Janna a big smile and took her groceries. He even stopped to write her a note that asked, "How are you today?" Janna smiled because someone was willing to communicate with her on her terms. She gave him the "thumbs up," and when he was done totaling up her groceries, he turned the display around and pointed to her total so she could see the numbers. Janna handed over her ATM card and he wrote down "credit or debit?" and Janna answered by pointing to the one she preferred to use.

Often cashiers decide the credit or debit question themselves when they find out you don't hear. After she paid, the cashier wrote "Have a good day" on his pad, and Janna left the store feeling good knowing she'd been treated as an equal customer, and it didn't take much extra effort on the part of that Whole Foods cashier to make her feel that way.

Deaf Norm #13: Variety is the Spice of Language

In the Introduction, we touched upon Pidgin Signed English (PSE), American Sign Language (ASL), and Signing Exact English (SEE), and we want to expand on the variety of language expressions a bit more here. A quick example: in SEE you would sign a sentence this way: "Do + you + want + soda?" In PSE, that sentence is signed "you + want + soda?" In ASL, that same sentence is signed "soda + you + want?" Many Deaf people have to use PSE daily because that is the most common form of signed language. Interpreters generally use PSE because it is the fastest kind of language to sign. But when Deaf are with Deaf, ASL rules.

One time we were at a political meet for the Deaf at New York University. The guest speaker was an elderly Deaf woman. Most Deaf people over the age of sixty went to an oral school where they were forced to use their voice and not use their hands. A lucky few were able to attend schools for the Deaf. Some older Deaf know only PSE or SEE because they were taught English by Hearing teachers. The focus on educating the Deaf using Deaf culture did not gain much mainstream popularity until the 1970s. So this elderly speaker at NYU began her lecture in PSE. Many people her age in the front row nodded as they understood and enjoyed her opening remarks. But there was a young woman, about fifteen years old, in the back row who leaned over to her friend and signed in ASL, "I don't understand her. She signs differently." The guest speaker saw what the young woman said, and she immediately changed her signing style from PSE to ASL and paused her lecture to ask us all, in ASL, "Can everyone here understand me?" When she received nods and waves of affirmation, she continued on with her lecture, about the history of Deaf rights in America. That sort of sensitivity is rare, but it's extremely important to try to provide when speaking to a culturally mixed group of signers.

Children of Deaf Adults

CODA stands for "Children of Deaf Adults"—Hearing children who were born to Deaf parents. These children are incredibly special because, from the moment they're born, they are bilingual. CODA babies have both the constant audible stimulus from the environment plus their parents' signing to them in ASL.

CODA kids grow up quickly. They are often forced into adult roles as negotiators and interpreters for their Deaf parents. That's a difficult role to play, but there are few people in the world able to so intimately communicate with each other as Deaf parents and their Hearing children. CODAs, bar none, make the best professional ASL interpreters. They are innately skilled, they care about Deaf culture and Deaf issues, and they know firsthand the heartbreak of being left out of a conversation or of not understanding everything in the world around them.

Many times the Deaf are called into action to interpret for Deaf friends and family, and all Deaf learn how to code-switch to find a variety of ways to communicate. If there's an emergency and the police or fire department or critical services are called in to assist a Deaf person, you'll often see a gang of friends and supporters gathering around the person in crisis to interpret for the Deaf person and for the emergency responders. Another example might be an interpreter friend who knows some Russian sign language and goes along to help interpret for a Deaf Russian couple at a doctor's appointment, with three languages in play: English from the doctor, English/Russian sign language from the interpreter, and Russian sign concepts from the Deaf couple. With all those languages being used in one visit, you can imagine how long it takes to make sure everyone understands each other. Finding a doctor willing to take the time to patiently explain everything is rare.

Janna Gets Caught Being Deaf

Janna refuses to be labeled hard of hearing by anyone, even though that was her medical evaluation growing up. That label has caused her a lot of trouble—she was not easily accepted by the Deaf community as "truly" Deaf because she could, at least according to her audiogram, hear a little bit. If Deaf people see her using her voice with Hearing people, she's labeled by the Deaf as hard of hearing. Janna is a proud Deaf person. She follows the Deaf norms because she culturally identifies with being Deaf. Janna no longer goes out with Hearing people who don't sign, because she doesn't want to pretend she understands what is being said. She did a lot of pretending growing up in Iowa and it was a depressing experience, because no matter how slowly people talked so that she could try to read their lips, they would all eventually forget that she was Deaf and would move their heads and talk over each other.

Janna, like a lot of Deaf children from Hearing families, hated the holidays because she felt totally left out of what was going on around her. Janna doesn't go home for the holidays to visit her Hearing family, and most of her Deaf peers also skip the family gatherings. It's better to be alone than to be left out. *Deaf* is not a bad word, and Janna will not pretend to be a Hearing person. If she doesn't hear something, that's okay. She's honest about what she hears and what she doesn't hear. She still needs Hearing people to look at her when they speak to her so that she can try to read their lips. She still needs to be tapped on the shoulder if you want her attention. Don't yell her name and expect her to respond.

Many Deaf people can "hear" with their ears, but they don't hear in the same way Hearing people hear. Sometimes Janna can hear a car horn honking. Sometimes she can hear voices behind her. Sometimes she can hear an airplane flying overhead. She doesn't always hear these things, because her attention and the noise level of the environment around her make "hearing" (sensing, really) difficult. Sometimes Janna uses a cellular phone to speak with David in an emergency. She does the talking, he does the listening. Janna also sometimes uses her voice on the telephone with her mother in Iowa because her mother is elderly and she grew up with Janna using her voice. Despite being able to use a cell phone and a regular phone, Janna still calls herself Deaf.

Janna went to high school at the Iowa School for the Deaf, but there was an option for her to be "mainstreamed" into Hearing schools where, for every class, she would have an interpreter, and all of her teachers and fellow students would be Hearing. Mainstreaming is popular because, the theory goes, the Deaf get used to dealing with the frustrations of the Hearing world. Janna is grateful she was able to attend a Deaf institute where all the students and teachers signed. Today, with the cochlear implantation of Deaf infants months after they are born, the trend for mainstreaming is on the rise, and Deaf institutes across the nation are closing their doors or merging with schools for the Blind.

There are many shades of Deafness. Even the Deaf can be insensitive in predetermining what a person can and cannot hear and who should be accepted as a "true" member of the Deaf community.

Deaf Norm #14: What Did You Call Me?

You've probably heard a lot of different names for Deaf people. In the 1930s and '40s, Deaf people were labeled deaf and dumb or deaf-mute. Those words still exist and are used by the uneducated, but you should never use those terms. Instead of saying deaf and dumb or deaf-mute, you can say "Deaf and does not speak." Deafie is also another word you should never use without permission. Some Deaf use it as a term of endearment, but if you use it without the proper permission or "cultural clearance," it'll be taken as a grave insult. "Profoundly Deaf" is also overused. Just say Deaf instead.

In the Hearing community today, many Deaf are labeled hearing impaired and the "impaired" part of that label suggests that they once had hearing or that they are somehow broken and need to be fixed by the medical community, as we discussed in the Introduction. Most Deaf people do not want to be called hearing impaired or even hard of hearing. A "hard of hearing" person is usually thought to be someone who spends most of their time in the mainstream Hearing community, has a lot of Hearing friends, and goes out socially with Hearing people to movies or dinner events. Many Deaf would not consider using "hard of hearing" to self-identify because they feel it is a negative description, but some Deaf prefer that label, so you can't assume to know what a person wishes to be called—you need to ask each Deaf person you meet how you should refer to them.

Deaf Norm #15: The Curse and Cure of Technology

Earlier in this chapter, we discussed how the Deaf are especially sensitive to flashing emergency lights while driving. That sensitivity to light makes its way into Deaf homes with a variety of attention-flashing devices.

Doorbell flashers are common in most Deaf homes. When a visitor rings the doorbell, a light in each room of the house flashes with a certain color to tell the Deaf which door the visitor is using. The front door might be a green light, the back door might be red, the garage door might be yellow, while the smoke alarm might be a clear light.

Deaf homes also have phone flashers that "ring" with light when the phone needs to be answered. The fancier setups tie in the phone to the other light system, so a flashing blue light might mean that the phone is ringing. Other homes might have a timing switch attached to a regular lamp that turns that light on and off as the phone rings.

There are also baby monitors that flash. You place the monitor in the baby's room and the receiver in the parents' room, and if the baby cries, lights flash to alert the parents.

Did you know that the "silent mode" vibration technology in pagers and cell phones was originally invented as a signaling device for the Deaf? In addition to using lights as alarms, the Deaf also use technologies that vibrate. Janna uses an alarm clock that shakes the bed like an earthquake.

When it first appeared, TDD (Telecommunication Device for the Deaf), or TTY (Teletypewriter for the Deaf), was a revolutionary device that allowed the Deaf to communicate with each other over standard telephone lines using regular telephones. Previously, getting in touch was an event, not a quick thought, and it took timing on both sides to meet. The TDD/TTY began life as a giant machine the size of a small refrigerator. You would type on giant keys and a machine-gun-loud printer would rattle your messages across humongous sheets of paper. Technology advanced, things got smaller and became portable, and the modern TDD/TTY was born. TDD/TTY communication works like this: you type on a small keyboard and what you type is transmitted via modemlike sounds across the phone lines to another TDD/TTY. What you type and what your friend types appear as scrolling words across each of your devices. If you're Hearing and you want to speak to a Deaf person who has a TTY, you can call the National Relay Service by dialing 711 from any phone, and a Hearing relay operator will type what you say to the Deaf person using a TTY and read back to you what the Deaf person types. Relay operators also allow the Deaf to easily call Hearing people, but that doesn't mean that the Hearing person will understand or accept the relay call. Often the Hearing hang up on relay operators before the communication process can be explained.

Videophones are the new TTY. You may have read about "videophones" over a decade ago, but those phones relied on a local dial-up connection and the images were chalky and fuzzy. Today's new videophones use high-speed Internet connections to present a crisp and clear real-time visual conversation between two Deaf people. Each user must have a videophone and an Internet IP address in order for the service to work. The traditional relay service the Deaf and Hearing currently use to communicate is now being supplemented—and in some areas replaced—by video relay where the Hearing call a special relay number and the video relay operator—who is fluent in ASL—uses a videophone to contact the Deaf person, who also has a videophone. The video relay call then becomes a real-time "interpreted" conversation in ASL and English or PSE. Everyone in the video relay loop is able to use their native language: the Deaf can use their eyes and hands to communicate and the Hearing can use their ears and voices.

Many of the younger Deaf today don't own TTY devices; they use alphanumeric text pagers. They carry on entire conversations using their pagers, and, unlike with the TTY machines, they don't need to worry about finding an AC outlet for power and they don't need to worry about missing a message. Pager technology has been a great leveler. The Deaf can communicate in real time with both Hearing and Deaf people without having to go through a third party.

The rise of the Internet has been a great help for Deaf communication. Chat rooms, instant messages, e-mail, and online communities can pop up anywhere. In cyberculture, no one knows and no one cares if you're Deaf.

Broadband Internet, via both DSL and cable, has provided even more techno-logical advances for the Deaf. Now you can make a "TTY" call that is fast and convenient via an Internet relay operator from your computer. Video-relay services are also on the rise, and they work when the Deaf, using a webcam or similar contraption, contacts a video interpreter online who then places a call and inter-prets for them. No typing is needed for video-relay service, and ASL is preserved with this technology.

Some Deaf have service animals to help them, in a kind of low-tech, highly trained way. Hearing dogs alert their owners to sounds around the home that may need attention. Janna has a cat named "Jack." Jack has learned that Janna is Deaf, and he communicates with her on her terms. When he wants to mewl at her for not having enough food in his dish, he will seek her out, lightly claw (tap) her on the forearm, and when she finally looks at him—*BLAM!*—she gets hit with a furious "meow" without any sound. Jack, when he talks to Janna, meows without voice. Janna has also learned how to read Jack. When he wants her to follow him, he will flip his curvy tail in a strange way (waving) that gets her attention, and he will not leave her alone until she follows. He has led her into the bathroom to show her that the water in the sink was left running. Another time he led her to the kitchen because the kettle was whistling. Janna also watches Jack to learn what direction a sound is coming from. If there is a siren or a firecracker or a thump, Jack will wake up and look in the direction of the sound, so Janna can get up and check it out for him. If someone knocks on the door instead of ringing the flashing light, Jack will walk to the door and sit in front of it to let her know that someone is on the other side. When David is home, Jack does not do these things because Jack will do nothing more than necessary; there are always naps that need taking.

Hearing aids are just that: aids. Hearing aids do not make a Deaf person Hearing. There are all kinds of hearing aids available. Most audiologists prefer the stronger behind-the-ear kind of aid, but some Deaf like to use the tiny ear-canal aid instead. As technology progresses and the size requirements of the aids shrink, a truly invisible and easily removable hearing aid will be on the horizon soon. Though the Deaf prefer the smallest possible hearing aids, audiologists may tell them that small is not the best kind of aid for them. Many times the traditional behind-the-ear hearing aids emit feedback, with a loud "EEEeeeeeee!" sound that

TTY Etiquette

If you ever use a TTY to communicate with the Deaf, or if you use a relay service to speak with the Deaf, there are a few things you need to keep in mind:

* Relay operators should remain transparent. Do not speak to them as vested participants in the conversation. Speak to the person you are calling. Don't say, "Ask them that," just ask your question, and the relay operator will handle the rest.

* Relay operators, like certified interpreters, are bound by a code of ethics to keep secrets. Your conversations should not be recorded or monitored without your knowledge.

* Do not interrupt. Wait until the other party is finished speaking.

* When you are finished speaking, type or say "GA," which is shorthand for "Go Ahead." That signals you are done and waiting for a reply.

* End the conversation by saying or typing "SK," which means "Stop Keying." Stop keying means you have nothing left to say and you are not going to type anything anymore.

* If you are feeling polite, you can try to wind up a conversation by saying or typing "GA or SK," which means you are either willing to continue chatting or you are ready to hang up.

* The reply might come back "GA," which means the other party wants to keep chatting.

* If the other party responds with "GA to SK," you can then end the conversation with your final thoughts by typing "SK SK," which means you are absolutely done and will have nothing more to say. The response to "SK SK" is to simply type "SK SK" back.

* If you are using a relay operator, it is always polite to thank the relay operator for helping after you end the conversation with your "SKs."

the Deaf can't hear but the Hearing certainly hear. You can always tap a Deaf person on the shoulder and make a handshape "E" sign near your ear to let them know their hearing aid is feeding back. Hearing aids make noise like that when the volume is turned up too loud.

Cochlear implants are a more permanent kind of hearing aid; they require major surgery. An electrical wire is inserted into the inner ear, and a computer outside the body decodes the environmental sounds and transmits them to the device implanted inside the head. Cochlear implant operations are irreversible, and the surgery destroys the cochlea. Most of the Deaf children born today are born to Hearing parents who want their children to be like them. Cochlear implant surgery is being performed earlier and earlier in a child's life. The decision to have the operation or not is taken away from the person receiving the surgery.

Cochlear implant devices do not allow the Deaf to hear. Cochlear implants are loud hearing aids and are a big issue in the Deaf community. Some Deaf feel that the implants steal Deaf children away from the community by "healing" their "broken" ears. The medical community sees implantation as another step in giving Deaf children every opportunity to live in the mainstream. No implant can change a culture, but all implants change the implanted. We've often seen children who've been implanted grow up to be outcasts in both the Deaf community and the Hearing world. Some in the Deaf community view the implanted as a kind of Frankenstein monster, while the Hearing community knows that the implanted aren't really Hearing.

We won't get into the firestorm over the implantation of Deaf infants with cochlear devices, except to say we could write an entire book on that topic. We believe all options should be explored by parents, with a full examination of the issues in the Deaf community and the medical community, and we implore everyone to do what is best for the child, not what is easiest for the parents. We ask all to accept the notion that Deafness is not a condition to be healed—it is a culture to be cherished.

Deaf Norm #16: Deaf and Hearing Must Remain Separate

There are some Deaf who believe the Deaf and the Hearing should live apart, because the Deaf in the Hearing culture can never claim all the things their own culture values because the Hearing majority will always win on policy, education, and recreation decisions. Those Deaf do not support the idea of intercultural mixing.

There are certain towns with "Deaf enclaves" where the Deaf can gather to support each other. Fredericksburg, Maryland, is one such town. Fredericksburg has a lot of Deaf families. Hearing people who work in the town know a lot of sign language, so if you are at the gas station or shopping mart or diner and you are Deaf, there is a great chance that the person serving you or helping you will know sign.

In May 2005, plans were announced to build an entire "Deaf friendly" town from scratch in South Dakota called Laurent, named after Deaf educator Laurent

The Deaf Gene

In the October 21, 2004, edition of *Nature* magazine, there was a report titled "Deaf by Design," and it examined a new trend in the Deaf community of identifying, via genetic testing in the fetal stage, whether a baby was Deaf or not. Since the Deaf community values Deaf children, Deaf parents, like their Hearing counterparts, want their children to be like them. Deaf parents want Deaf children. Genetic testing can now reveal changes in genes for proteins connexin 26 and connexin 30, which influence how effectively the cochlea will process sounds. These genetic protein tests reveal whether the fetus has the "Deaf gene" or not.

Clerc. Anyone can live in Laurent, South Dakota, but you better know sign language if you want to prosper. Laurent is a town built by the Deaf for the Deaf, and there are already 153 families and single folk from 33 states who have paid for lots in the town. Janna loves the idea of a "Deaf town," where the Deaf are the majority and the Hearing follow Deaf norms.

You'll also see Deaf clustering in apartment buildings. Often, no one locks their doors, so people can come and go as they please in and out of each other's apartments. Deaf parties, if you have yet to attend one, are incredibly LOUD, and that surprises a lot of Hearing people because they don't think the Deaf can hear. Remember, sounds are vibrations, and if you turn up the volume and pump the bass, you are going to feel the music beating through your body. If you're Hearing and you're going to a Deaf party, be sure to wear earplugs to protect your ears from sound damage.

There are some Deaf who believe the Deaf should date and marry the Deaf and not mix with Hearing people. Janna is Deaf and David is Hearing, and while there are some communication and cultural differences that need to be overcome every now and then, we do not believe separation from the mainstream is particularly desirable. We need to find a way to communicate with each other beyond labels and the stratification of cultures so that we may begin to till the common ground of our shared humanity. We don't care what other people think, because true love conquers all.

Communication Breakdowns & Misunderstandings

Communication breakdowns can lead to hurtful misunderstandings that may lead to anger and mistrust. Here are some common communication breakdowns between the Deaf and the Hearing and how to prevent them from happening.

* Hearing people forget that Deaf people need to read lips. Hearing people often talk without eye contact with the Deaf person. Sometimes people are talking

to other people on a hidden cellular phone or just talking to themselves. The solution is that if you want to talk to a Deaf person, look at them and keep your lips toward them, especially if you have a Deaf coworker or friend.

* In ASL you use the handshape "6" for the number, but that handshape "6" is also a manual alphabet "W" and, to Hearing people, the handshape "6" is how they make the numeral "3" with their fingers. When an ASL-speaking Deaf person wants to order the #6 combo, the Hearing cashier always gives them the #3 combo, or, if they know a little bit of sign, the cashier gets confused and asks, "What is a 'W' combo?" The solution is for the Deaf to remember to hold up all five fingers on one hand and one finger on the other hand so that the Hearing person will be able to "see" the number six.

* Sometimes Hearing people assume the Deaf are helpless. If you see a Deaf person writing to someone, you don't have to rush over to help or voice or interpret. The solution is to help only if asked.

* Hearing people think that if they point to something, they're communicating. Here's an example: you're at a picnic and you're the only Deaf person there. Twelve people around you have their mouths stuffed full with hotdogs. One person taps you on the shoulder and points to something across the table. Their mouth is full of hotdog, and they mouth something at you. You don't know if they want a napkin, a bottle of mustard, potato chips, or what. The solution is to always follow your mother's advice and never speak OR POINT with your mouth full, and to ask for something only when you can clearly indicate what you are requesting.

* Signing can be dangerous! When Deaf people have a conversation, it can get heated and aggressive, with hands, fists, and arms flying everywhere. If one Deaf person signs "so what" about a negative experience, it looks a lot like the Italian gesture of taking a flat hand and flipping it out from under your

chin. The signs are exactly the same, but the movements have different cultural meanings. The solution is to choose your signs carefully, because you never know who is watching you.

* The Deaf are not personal sign language tutors who work free. If you want a Deaf friend, that's great, but don't use the friendship just to learn sign. The solution is that if you want to learn sign, offer to pay for the lessons.

* Do not exaggerate your speech if you must use your voice with a Deaf person. Deaf people are taught to read and interpret lips based on normal word pronunciation. Don't do any r-e-a-l-l-y s-l-o-w p-r-o-n-u-n-c-i-a-t-i-o-n-s, because you will not be understood. The solution is to speak how you naturally speak, but slow down just a little bit, because many Hearing people naturally speak really fast.

* If you don't know a sign, don't start finger spelling. Write or mime or make understandable gestures. Don't rely on trying to become a Rochester Method expert, because finger spelling is rarely used in ASL.

* Don't stare at Deaf people signing. If you stare at the Deaf signing on the subway or on the street, be prepared to get an eyeful back.

* If you are at a Deaf event where everyone knows some sort of sign language, feel free to start up a conversation, because there is no need for an interpreter. If someone tries to interpret for you because you are a newbie, the solution is to kindly decline the offer, because in order to improve you need to learn from your own mistakes.

Maybe This *IS* a Textbook

Earlier, in the Introduction, we said this book was not a textbook. But we *are* teachers of American Sign Language and reserve the right to give you pop quizzes, so pull out your pencils and prepare to practice what we've preached.

DEAF CULTURE POP QUIZ

Pick the best answer or answers to the following questions:

1 **What do you do to get a Deaf person's attention?**

a) tap shoulder

b) tap on head

c) tap arm

d) a & c

e) a & b

f) all of above

ANSWER: **D.** You tap on the shoulder or the arm to get a Deaf person's attention.

2 **What are the appropriate terms for people with hearing loss who use and practice Deaf norms?**

a) hearing impaired

b) deaf-mute

c) deaf

d) Deaf

e) deaf and dumb

ANSWER: **D**. The Deaf community uses the "Big D" for "Deaf" because it is more than just a word. "Big D" Deaf stands for a culture of values that are separate from just being "deaf."

3 You are at a crowded Deaf party and you see two people signing. You need to get to the other side of the room by walking between them. You:

   a) stand and wait until they are done talking.

   b) go through them—gently.

   c) tap on one signer's shoulder and move through.

   d) bend down where you do not interrupt their conversation and crouch as you walk by.

ANSWER: **B**. Just go! Don't hang around. Don't wait. Certainly don't crouch down so you don't "bother" the signers, because your crouching is more bothersome than if you were to just pass by and sign "excuse me" as you pass.

4 Deaf people "hear" with...

   a) their eyes.

   b) their bodies.

   c) their hands.

   d) their interpreters.

ANSWER: **A**. The Deaf use their eyes to hear. The other choices help give form to the environment, but "hearing" is done through the eyes.

5 All Deaf people can read lips:

   a) 50 percent of the time.

   b) 80 percent of the time.

   c) 25 percent of the time.

   d) none of the above.

ANSWER: **D**. We don't have a firm answer on what percentage of Deaf people can read lips. Don't rely on the Deaf reading your lips to be fully understood. Sign or write or mime or gesture to even the communication field.

6 **ASL, as used by the Deaf, is:**

a) the same as English.

b) similar to French.

c) similar to Spanish.

d) similar to Italian.

ANSWER: **B**. Gallaudet and Clerc invented American Sign Language, and Clerc's native French influenced the construction of the language, including its grammar and syntax.

7 **You're at a Deaf event and you're talking to a group. You need to go to the bathroom. You:**

a) leave and go to the bathroom.

b) tell everyone in the room that you are going to the bathroom.

c) tell the group you are talking with that you are leaving to go to the bathroom.

d) draw a map that shows where you are about to go before you leave.

ANSWER: **C**. You should always let your group know where you're going...even if it is to get another drink or to go find something you left outside in your car.

8 **Deaf people use ASL because:**

a) there is no other language that is so visual.

b) they are not interested in learning English.

c) it is an innate way to communicate.

d) they like the attention they get from Hearing people when they sign in public.

ANSWER: **C**. Deaf people have a natural ability to "speak" ASL as infants, much in the same way Hearing children have the ability to speak their native tongue. Hearing babies babble with their voices while Deaf babies babble with their hands.

9 **How do most Deaf people wake up in the morning?**

a) They use their parents or children as human alarm clocks.

b) They use a special alarm clock that has flashing lights or a vibrating alarm.

c) They train dogs or cats to wake them up at a certain time.

d) They stay awake all night on days they need to wake up early.

ANSWER: **B**. Flashing lights and vibrating alarms are the preferred ways to wake up in the morning.

10 **When you arrive at a Deaf event you should:**

a) shake hands with everyone.

b) wave at people and wait until after the event to talk to them.

c) hug everyone.

d) call out people's names so that they know you see them.

ANSWER: **C**. Hugging is big both coming and going in the Deaf community, and the hugs are not light wraparounds. The hugs are more "bear hug" than friendly embrace.

Sometimes Signing is Sloppy

One of our favorite things to do with our ASL students is to throw a "dinner party" during class, where everyone must pick up a plate piled with pretzels or potato chips with one hand and a giant cup of soda with the other hand and then mingle while eating, drinking, and signing in ASL with everyone else in the class. The hook to the assignment is that your plate of food and your drink must never leave control of your body: you may not set them down on a desk, table, or chair, or ask anyone else to hold them for you. You are also not allowed to spill any food or drink on the floor, or you will have to clean up after everybody else when the party is over.

It is quite a sight to see these brilliant students struggling to make textbook-perfect ASL signs with a potato chip hanging out of their mouth and soda spilling down their arm, but that is the point of the exercise: welcome to the world of the Deaf! Those "spilling while you chat" issues are exactly what the Deaf face every day, and you need to find a way to make that experience common. ASL is not perfect. Sometimes signing is sloppy. Sometimes you don't sign like you see in the book, and that's okay. Sometimes your hands are full, but you gotta find a way to sign anyway! Sometimes two-handed signs are made with one hand against an imagined second hand in the air. The clever students balance their soda cup on a raised knee for a moment. Some try to balance the plate on top of the cup, or vice-versa, and sign with only one hand. All of those are smart and acceptable solutions for finding creative ways to sign.

Don't
2 Make that
Face at Me!

Facial expression is important in creating good American Sign Language sentences and ideas. In ASL, facial expressions fulfill a mechanical and structural role for communication, because the face offers clues to whether the person talking is angry or happy or confused, or whether the person had a good or bad experience. The cool thing is that facial expression is easy to learn, because, without knowing it, you have most likely made these "faces" hundreds of times over the course of your life.

Early learners of ASL sometimes get stuck in focusing only on hands—that's a habit you must break early. Imagine an invisible square around a person that crosses their torso and extends beyond both arms and a foot above the person's head. That is the "ASL field of view" you must become comfortable watching as people sign, because that entire square will be filled with clues to meaning and intent. You must watch hands, arm movements, facial expressions, speed of signing, relation of hands to face and torso, and lip movements. All those factors must blend together as you speak ASL and as you watch someone speaking ASL. Getting it right takes a lot of time and practice. Don't stare at one spot or you'll miss 90 percent of the meaning. You need to relax your eyes—letting them glaze over a bit for the "big view"—and take in the entire square and what's floating in it to do really well as an ASL learner.

Here are the most commonly used ASL facial expressions. We will refer back to these in the coming chapters when you start to learn sentences and expressive exclamations.

✳ NEGATIVE

One of the most common facial expressions is "negative." Move your eyebrows downward with your head slightly down and moved forward a bit. Cock your head to the side a little for an extra pinch of attitude. Use this facial expression to convey "confused," "suspicious," "frustrated," "jealous," "don't like," "don't want," or "never."

✳ POSITIVE

"Positive" is another very common facial expression. Lift your eyebrows up a bit, lifting your head slightly so your chin is just a shade above level, and smile a wee bit if the mood suits you. Use this facial expression to show "confidence," "conceited" (even a "positive" facial expression can have a negative connotation!), "happy," "hope," "enjoy," or "like."

✳ FEEL THE CHA

One of our favorite facial expressions is "cha." Make it by silently saying "cha" without much more than the sound of air coming out of your mouth. Make your eyes huge and wide open, lift your eyebrows, and leave your mouth open after pronouncing "cha." Your hands are indicating the gigantic size of something, like a "massive building" or "huge muscles" or a "tall person" or even "big boobs." Show with your hands and arms how humongous the thing is you are describing, and you "feel the cha!"

Blowing Air

Dizzy Gillespie, the trumpet player, was famous for billowing out his cheeks like a croaking frog while he played his instrument. That kind of cheek action is what you need to "blow air" in ASL to indicate great distance or a lengthy passing of time. Show with your arms and hands the amount of time that has passed or space traveled, like "far away," "far up in the air," "long hallway," or "all day."

✳ TONGUE ME!

Despite what your mother taught you, sticking out your tongue in ASL is an important part of communication, and if you stick it out, STICK IT OUT, and don't be shy about showing a little pink! You use the "tongue me" facial expression by sticking out your tongue, lowering your eyebrows, and looking a bit disgusted. This facial expression conveys negative ideas, like "not yet," "disgusted," or "never seen before."

✳ WH-QUESTION

The "wh-question" is one of the most important facial expressions you'll learn, and students have a hard time getting this one right. It takes a lot of practice to create the "wh-question" in the right context. Press your eyebrows downward hard while you tilt your head forward a nudge and to the side. Use this facial expression at the end of an ASL sentence as punctuation to indicate that you're asking a question by pausing for a moment at the end of your sentence when you're asking something that requires an answer. Use this facial expression for questions that begin with "wh," like "who?" "where?" "why?" "what?" and also for "how much?" "how many?" and "how come?" Don't sweat any of this! We'll go over it again and again in the chapters to come.

✳ YES/NO QUESTION

Like the "wh-question" facial expression, the "yes/no question" facial expression requires a pause at the end of a sentence to indicate that you're waiting for a "yes" or "no" response. Move your eyebrows up and hunch your shoulders slightly forward to indicate that you're expecting an answer. Open your mouth a bit so that your upper teeth are visible between your lips. Cock your head to the side a little to further indicate that you're waiting for an answer. Use this facial expression to ask questions like "Are you Deaf?" "Do you live in New York?" "Do you wanna go out for a drink?"

✳ BORED TO DEATH

"Bored to death" has a plethora of uses, and it can be an effective end to a conversation when used by itself without any sign. Tilt your head down a bit and make your face "dead." By "dead," we don't mean blank or expressionless. "Dead" means you purposefully make your eyes droopy, crinkle down the edges of your mouth, and tilt your head to the side as if you're nodding off into the Land of the Dead. Use this facial expression to show "boredom," "geez," "oh no," or "yeah, right." Here's an example of how the "bored to death" facial expression can show both context and location at the same time: if you say in English, "I sat all day—what a drag," that would translate into ASL like this: when you sign "sit," you repeat that word over and over, indicating that you were doing the same thing all day. The ASL structure then breaks down into all-day + sit + sit + sit, and your facial expression should be actively zombielike.

✷ SHOCK THE MONKEY

"Shock the monkey" is a great facial expression that we sometimes call the "boing!" reaction. You create this face by thinking "*BOING!*" to yourself and then reacting to the "boing!" as if you'd been shocked with a cattle prod. Quickly blink your eyelids and then, keeping your eyes wide open, open your mouth a bit as you sorta sneer with one corner of your mouth, while straining your neck muscles. This facial expression is used to indicate "surprised," "oh really?" "whoa!" "shocked," or "oh no!"

✷ NO

The "no" facial expression is one you'll use a lot because it helps in indicating negation and your determined will not to do something. Unlike with the "yes/no question" facial expression, you're not waiting for a response to a question—you're responding "no." Shake your head a few times, glower with your eyebrows down as far as they'll go, draw down your mouth, and turn your head a bit, as if thinking, "Whatchu talkin' 'bout, Willis?" The "no" facial expression indicates "no," "not," "nada," "nothing," "not here," "nope," "don't like," or "don't want."

Practice Makes Perfect Faces

Here are some quick tips to help you make the best possible facial expressions:

✱ Practice with a mirror.

✱ Videotape your face close up and critique your performance.

✱ Quiz your friends by asking them to identify your facial expression.

✱ Raise and drop only one eyebrow at a time.

✱ Lift and lower one corner of your mouth.

✱ Squint one eye and then the other.

✱ Strain your neck so that you can see the muscles under the skin.

✱ Think of every emotion you can and make a facial expression for each, holding it two seconds before moving on to the next one.

✱ When you read a book or the newspaper or watch a television commercial, copy the facial expressions of the actors on TV or express how you imagine the people in the story/article feel.

✱ You can use the old mime's trick of moving your flat hand up and down in front of your face and changing your face from happy to sad to excited to depressed with each pass of your hand, and have your friends and family guess each expression.

3 You Want a Pizza or a Lesbian?

et's get you ready for some of the curious cultural and regional differences you may encounter in American Sign Language. Signed languages around the world have their own accents, regional customs, international issues of proper name sign ownership, country dialects, and non-universal mime and gestures. This chapter is an introduction to the issues and ideas that will be covered throughout the rest of the book. We'll spice this chapter with some handshape references—don't worry, we'll get into them more in the next chapter.

We'll also break down a couple of sentences so you can see how an English sentence translates into an ASL-structured language. Later in the book, we'll translate with you from English to ASL step by step.

When we lived in the Midwest, we didn't know the sign for "pizza" was awfully close to that of "lesbian" in New York. It was strange when we moved to New York and went out with Deaf friends and we signed in ASL "we're hungry for pizza" (us-two + hungry + for-for + pizza), only to be met with peals of laughter as our new friends pointed at us and said, "You just said you wanted to eat a lesbian!" (You + duh + peabrain + you + eat + lesbian?) We looked at each other and realized we had a lot to learn in New York.

Here are some other differences in regional signs to give you an idea of how easy miscommunication can be between the Deaf, let alone the Hearing, as they travel beyond the cultural safety of their hometowns.

You can find all these handshapes at the end of Chapter 4, and also on the inside flaps of the cover, if you are so inclined to stumble through all these ASL concepts right now. Our preference, though, is to let all of this wash over you for the moment. Just read the descriptions and try to connect them to the illustrations. Worry about actually creating these handshapes and signs later. You can always come back and practice these signs after you've read Chapter 4.

✴ A NEW YORK LESBIAN

The sign for "lesbian" in New York uses the manual alphabet handshape "L." Hold a hand—either hand—in front of your chin and lightly tap your "L" hand on your chin twice. The "L" here stands for the L in "lesbian."

The sign for "lesbian" in the Midwest is the manual alphabet "G" with the index finger and thumb touching the chin. You see that sign in New York as well, but it's more specific to gay men, while in the Midwest it's more universally applied to mean gay for either gender.

✴ A MIDWESTERN PIZZA

The sign for "pizza" in the Midwest uses the same manual alphabet handshape "L" as does the New York lesbian sign, but instead of tapping the "L" on your chin, you crisply create the sign four to five inches away from your chin and slightly shake your hand back and forth twice. In this sign, the "L" indicates the crust side of your pizza slice—you're "holding" the pizza in your hand and are about to place it in your mouth. The confusion came when we signed "pizza" in our fast and sloppy Midwestern way and were misunderstood by our New York Deaf friends, who thought we were trying to order lesbians.

In New York, the sign for pizza is putting a handshape "Flat B" in front of your mouth with your fingers pointing at your teeth. Your hand is the slice of pizza.

✳ A NEW YORK DOG

The sign for "dog" in New York is created by using a handshape "Flat B." Tuck it behind your ear and then, like a dog scratches at a flea, "flip" your lower earlobe twice.

✳ A MIDWESTERN DOG

This sign might look familiar. To sign "dog" in the Midwest, you do it in two steps. It's a direct use of the "come here" dog training command you may have seen or may even use in your own life.

Step ❶

Pat your handshape "Flat B" on your upper thigh, then raise your hand up to shoulder level, and when you reach the top of your shoulder...

Step ❷

...snap your fingers! The sign is just that simple.

Which sign is better? Which sign is clearer or more universal? It doesn't matter, really, because, unlike the "lesbian"/"pizza" debacle, if you are from the Midwest or New York or China or California, you'll recognize and understand these universal gestures for dog.

✳ A NEW YORK
YOU'RE WELCOME

Make a "Bent B" handshape with the palm facing upward and positioned in the space a foot away from the center of your torso. Slowly bring your hand toward your torso and stop an inch away from your belly button.

    This sign pattern is exactly the same for "introduction." It's common in ASL that a sign can have several different meanings depending on context. So it's not enough to just memorize the movement of the sign, you also need to know if there are any synonyms for the sign you're using. This sign may also look a lot like the universal gesture for "come on over" — it's the same idea as "you're welcome." The context of this "you're welcome" sign is as a response to "thank you."

✳ A MIDWESTERN
YOU'RE WELCOME

In the Midwest, "you're welcome" looks totally different. You create a "W" hand-shape and start the sign below your ear, near your cheek. Arc the "W" out from your cheek a foot or so into the space in front of you. If you were a Deaf New Yorker and moved to the Midwest and saw this sign for the first time, you most likely wouldn't understand the sign based on context alone, and you'd have to ask what that sign meant. If you ever see a sign you don't recognize, try to repeat the sign to the person who signed it, raise your shoulders and eye-brows and shake your head a couple of times, and that should make it clear to the signer that you're requesting a definition.

America, "The Filthy"

Now we're getting into the touchy subject of reconciling international signs with American Sign Language, which can be hard to do, what with political correctness issues and the hard-won rights of the Deaf to speak their own language in their own blunt, visual way. Older ASL signs for countries were built mainly on unique (some might say stereotypical) physical features that do not play well in today's politically correct world. There was resistance in the Deaf community to change the ASL signs to be more politically correct, because the community saw it as an outside invasion violating the Deaf language. Over the past few years, a sort of truce has been supported in the ASL community to change some of the older, culturally insensitive signs into more meaningful and useful ones. The standard agreement now when it comes to signs of nationality is that the Deaf from the "home country" can decide the sign for their own country, and those new "home signs" should become the accepted standard for communication. That said, you may see older Deaf who are either unaware of the new nationality signs or prefer to use the original ASL signs they grew up using. In some cases, matters of insensitivity and being politically correct are of no interest to them, because the only important thing is to preserve the original sign vocabulary of ASL, even if it later becomes outdated or appears intolerant.

An interesting example is the ASL sign for "America." Both hands are intertwined in front of the torso in a modified "clenched praying" position. A horizontal circle is made twice in front of the body. That sign means "together," but, outside of America, that isn't the sign used for "America." The international sign for America is the back of a flat hand under the chin with fingers wiggling and waving. That sign means "filthy," and plays right into the stereotype in some countries that people from the United States are "filthy Americans." Now you can see why using the country of origin's sign as the international sign name for that country is a good policy that can preserve the home country's honor and reputation. Here are a few other examples of older ASL signs and the newly accepted signs invented in the country of origin.

✳ FILIPINO THE OLD WAY

The old ASL sign for "Filipino" was using a manual alphabet handshape "P" (for Philippines) and then "cutting" it downward in strokes across the back of your other hand as if you were slicing a loaf of bread.

✳ FILIPINO THE NEW WAY

The new way to sign "Filipino," as created by Deaf Filipinos, is made in three steps. This sign suggests the visual beauty of traditional Filipino clothes.

STEP ❶

Begin the sign by taking handshape "Fist" and placing it at the edge of your opposite shoulder.

STEP ②

Open your hand in the numerical handshape "4" by making your fingers open and close as you move your hand down your shoulder a bit. You're creating a "puffy sleeve"— you may not have limber enough fingers to make this sign look beautiful, but if you practice it in a mirror, you'll quickly learn how to create the "cascading fingers" look of this part of the sign.

STEP ③

The final part of the sign is to close the handshape "4" on your lower shoulder/upper arm.

✳ AUSTRALIA THE OLD WAY

The old ASL sign for "Australia" is made in two steps, suggesting an Australian outback hat with one side flipped up.

STEP ❶

Start the sign with the handshape "B" over your eyebrow as if you're about to salute. Your hand is the brim of the Australian outback hat.

STEP ❷

Next, flip your hand out and up so that your palm is now facing the sky. This movement is almost like a salute, except instead of moving your handshape "B" straight out, you flip your palm out, up, and over a bit to indicate the flipped brim of the hat.

✳ AUSTRALIA THE NEW WAY

The sign the Deaf in Australia have for their home country is also created using two steps, but the idea of the sign is quite different from the Outback hat. This sign for Australia suggests a joey, or baby kangaroo, being removed from the mother kangaroo's pouch.

STEP ❶

Place both hands near your hips in the numerical handshape "8" position in which the tips of your thumbs make a circle by connecting to the tips of your middle fingers.

STEP ❷

Next, move your arms up and outward in an arc away from your body, as if you're lifting something sort of heavy. At the end of your arc, open your numerical handshape "8" middle fingers outward, as if you're letting go of something. You've just removed a baby roo from your pouch and released it into the world.

This new sign for Australia is one of our all-time favorite country signs, because it's visual, cultural, beautiful, and fun to make, and the sign is so universal and cute that many people from a variety of countries get it on the first try.

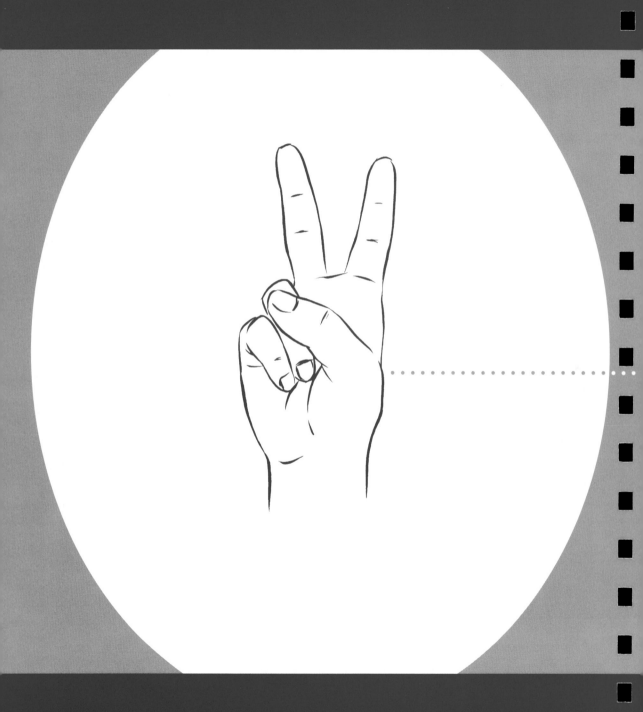

Part Two

Throwing Down the Signs

4 Form that Handshape

Handshapes are the best and fastest way to learn American Sign Language. The manual alphabet, while made of handshapes, is used for finger spelling the proper names of people, cities, other named locations, and states. Handshapes serve as synonyms in ASL, so you learn them once and then use them over and over again. Handshapes and facial expressions help students learn ASL via the "whole body" approach. There are more than fifty handshapes in ASL. Here we demonstrate the ten most common and most commonly misunderstood. All ten of the handshapes you'll learn in this chapter will be used throughout the rest of this book. We've given them names to help you remember them. At the end of this chapter, we've included the twenty-six manual alphabet signs and the first ten numbers.

Handshape "1": The Eye Poker

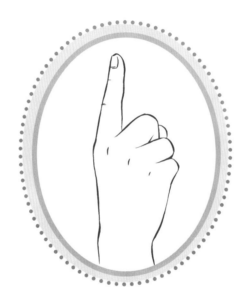

Our first handshape is "1," or, as we like to remember it, the eye poker—a favorite of small children. It's the numerical handshape for the number one, and, as you can see, it's also the universal gesture of sports fans everywhere: "We're Number One!"

Always

The sign for "always" uses handshape "1" and is created by raising your hand to shoulder level, pursing your lips, and making a small circle twice on the horizontal plane with your hand. To emphasize, move your torso and shoulder as you make the circle and put your body into it each time you create one circle pass.

Lonely

"Lonely" is actually a lot of fun to sign because you get to let "woe is me" seep through your finger, and you get to make a pretty, pouty mouth. Take your handshape "1" hand and touch the side of the finger on your chin twice in a downward movement. You can even tilt your head to the side a bit and let tears well up in your eyes for a really great effect.

Walking along

You can also use handshape "1" to create movement and action, as demonstrated in the sign for "walking along." Here's how to take your previously lonely index finger out on the town in three simple steps!

STEP ❶

Your lips are pursed as if you're getting ready to pronounce the word "walk," but you never finish the full pronunciation. Start this sign by taking your eye-poker finger and moving it out a foot or so from your shoulder.

STEP ❷

Next, move your handshape "1" across your body twice in a "walking" movement.

Step ❸

Finally, on the third and final "walk," rest your handshape "1" for a moment in midair and make eye contact with the person you're talking with to make sure they understood who and/or what was walking where. They'll let you know whether they understand you or not. That lonely finger might represent you, your friend, or a stranger.... The context of the entire sentence defines exactly whom that lonely handshape is representing.

Handshape "B": The Karate Chop

There are several handshapes in ASL that use a flat palm, but sometimes that palm is bent or the position of the thumb is slightly different. It's important to know the difference between the handshape styles for a flat palm versus those for a modified palm. For handshape "B," the karate chop, make a flat palm, with your thumb bent across your palm. Handshape "B" is the shape for the letter B in the manual sign alphabet. Hai-ya!

Blue

Put your hand in the "karate chop" position, as if you're going to strike someone with the flat edge of your palm, but instead of karate chopping, just twist your handshape "B" back and forth at the wrist an inch or two each way twice on the horizontal plane. Your arm doesn't move, only your wrist moves to make the sign. Your facial expression is neutral, and your lips are configured to begin to pronounce the word *blue*.

Boston

Boston is one of the few cities in America—Chicago, New York, and Philadelphia are others—that has a sign name instead of a finger spelled name. Over the course of the following three steps, your facial expression will be neutral, but your lips over the three steps will form a semi-pronunciation of Boston as "Bah," in which each letter in "Bah" is pronounced in sequence with the steps.

STEP 1

Begin with your handshape "B" at shoulder level in front of your face, with palm facing away from you. Keep your elbow near your side.

STEP 2

Move your handshape "B" away from your shoulder on a horizontal plane to the right if you're right-handed, or the reverse if you're left-handed.

STEP ❸

When your hand is out past your shoulder and directly above your elbow, finish the sign by moving your handshape "B" back in toward your body at a 45-degree diagonal angle downward toward your waist. Remember, these steps are all done in one fluid, non-stop motion.

Painting the wall

The handshape "B" is also used to describe something being painted. In this sign, your fingers become the bristles of the brush, and your facial expression is neutral.

STEP 1

Raise your handshape "B" "paintbrush" so that your palm is on the same plane as your head. Your elbow sticks out a bit, away from your body.

STEP 2

Bend your wrist as if you're painting a wall with the tips of your fingers. Your arm should also move, to give the sign a natural flow. Repeat the painting movement a few times to get the message across.

STEP 3

Complete the sign by leaving your hand bent at the wrist. This is a less formal approach to making this sign, so you don't have to always end up exactly where you began in step one.

Handshape "Flat B": The Bitch Slap

The handshape "Flat B"—the bitch slap—isn't part of the manual sign alphabet, but it's a handshape you'll use a lot. Notice how, in "Flat B" mode, the thumb is not cocked over the palm; the thumb is flat against the side of the palm, as if you were going to "bitch slap" someone. That is the major and important difference between the "Flat B" and the plain "B" handshapes.

Forget

The "forget" sign looks as if you're wiping away your memory or wiping sweat from your brow. Notice how this handshape "Flat B" has the thumb extended away from the rest of the hand. It's still considered the "Flat B" handshape because the thumb's still in the same plane as the palm.

STEP 1

Position your hand in front of your forehead to begin the sign. Your hand should be an inch or so away from your head.

STEP 2

Now "wipe" away your memory by moving your hand across your forehead—without actually touching your forehead—and then end with your fingers curled into your palm while your thumb remains erect.

Lecture

To sign "lecture" with the handshape "Flat B," raise your handshape so that it's parallel with your head with your palm facing the side of your head. Your elbow is angled out away from your body. Make the sign by doing a couple of tiny, gentle, little Judo chop motions of an inch or two.

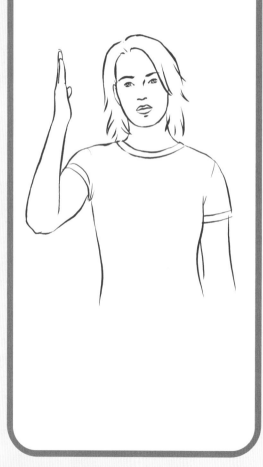

Napkin

"Napkin" also uses the handshape "Flat B," in two steps. Bend your palm just a little bit, so it'll fit against your face, but don't cup your palm too much.

STEP

Place your "Flat B" on one corner of your mouth. Your "Flat B" has become your napkin, and you need to dab away some spaghetti sauce from your lips.

STEP **2**

Move your "Flat B" to the other side of your mouth to catch the extra splash of sauce with your "napkin."

Handshape "A"

Handshape "A" is the manual sign alphabet for the letter *A*, and, like our handshape "B" and "Flat B" friends before, the position of the thumb is vital to the creation of this hand-shape. The thumb is not connected to the fist; the thumb is erect on the side of the fist. There's a handshape coming soon in this chapter called "Fist," where the thumb bends over the fingers to create a tight fist, but that's not what we're doing here with handshape "A." So remember, an "A" does not a fist make.

Going back and forth

ASL is wonderful for visually telling stories about traveling across time and distance. One example of this is the sign for "going back and forth," in which your entire body gets dragged along by your handshape "A."

STEP 1

The first step in "going back and forth" is to give yourself the "thumbs up!" sign, and once you've done that and positioned your hand in front of your torso, you'll be ready to begin your journey.

STEP 2

Move your handshape "A" across your body on a horizontal plane to the other shoulder. Move your torso back and forth a bit as you repeat this "traveling" from shoulder to shoulder, twice. You can even put your shoulders into the sign, as you make them rise and fall over the exhausting journey. Make sure your facial expression matches the tone of your journey. If your travel was easy, show that with a positive face. If your road was rocky and exhausting, use a negative facial expression.

Sauce

Remember the spaghetti sauce you wiped from the corner of your mouth with your "Flat B" handshape napkin? Here's where you got that spaghetti sauce!

Step ❶

Turn handshape "A" upside down from the way you used it in "going back and forth" and place it at the center of your torso. Your elbow is angled away from your torso. This sign looks like the universal gesture for "thumbs down," and you can certainly think of it that way. You can also think of your thumb as being either the sauce pouring out of the can or the wooden spoon that's stirring the sauce already in the pan.

Step ❷

"Stir" or "pour" your handshape "A" in a small circle on a horizontal plane in front of your imaginary saucepan. Have your facial expression match your feelings about stirring the pot.

Handshape "Claw"

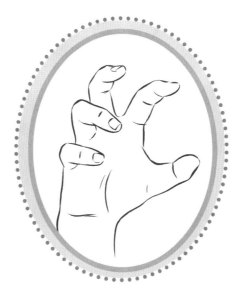

Handshape "Claw" is one of great power, menace, and beauty! The "Claw" requires a rigid hand, so don't be lazy when making it. Let your entire palm arch inward when you show the evil fingers of death!

Freckles

Creating "freckles" is your first two-handed sign! Make both of your hands into "Claw" handshapes, and bring them to your cheeks or your arms or your chest or wherever you want to describe freckles, and touch that area a few times. We chose the face for our example. Dot your face with your "Claw" fingertips to indicate freckles. Your "freckle dotting" should match the amount of freckles you're describing.

Monster

Being a monster takes two hands, too! Make both hands into "Claw" hand-shapes. Stick out your elbows. Raise your shoulders. Lower your brow. Create a frightening facial expression that will make little children scream! Make a guttural sound. Cock back your "Claws" at the wrists, then snap them forward as you growl again. Now, if you're feeling daring, you could combine both "monster" and "freckles" to create a super-scary "freckled monster!"

Hot

Handshape "Claw" also indicates when you or the temperature is hot. This is not the sign you use to indicate food that is "hot" and spicy or that guy or gal who's "hot" and sexy. We'll get to the "hot and sexy" sign later, in the morally bankrupt Chapter 11.

STEP 1

Make an agitated facial expression— open your mouth as if saying "hot" and form your evil "Claw" smack-dab in front of your mouth.

STEP 2

Quickly turn your "Claw" handshape outward into the center space in front of your body by twisting your wrist. Keep the "Claw" firm and intact at all times. The only movement in this sign happens at the wrist. Your "Claw" palm faces outward.

Radio

Bring your handshape "Claw" next to your ear. Position your elbow outward from your body and purse your lips a bit as part of your facial expression. Twist your wrist a few times, as if you were turning the knob on an old-fashioned radio dial.

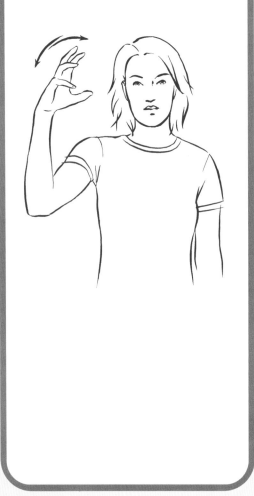

Handshape "Fist"

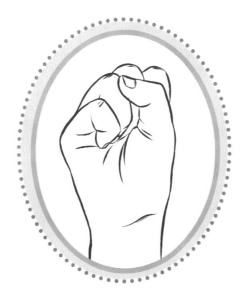

Handshape "Fist" is also the manual alphabet letter for "S." We prefer to call it "Fist" because it's more visual and easier to remember how to make. Make your handshape "Fist" strong and tight so that your movements will be crisp and clear.

Driving

You'll probably recognize this sign for "driving" as a universal gesture, and it is, but here's how to sign it in ASL. Tilt your head back as if you have the top down and the wind is blowing through your hair. Your facial expression is positive—you're dreaming of the open road. Take your handshape "Fist"—you can use one "Fist" or two—grab the "steering wheel" in front of you, and steer your car or boat or golf cart or whatever by moving your "Fist" across your body in a series three times.

Stupid

Sometimes when the Deaf make the sign for "stupid," they're in a heightened emotional state, and, even after years of practice, they smack themselves in the forehead a little too hard because you rarely call *yourself* stupid—you usually use this sign to tell someone else they're stupid. So when you create your handshape "Fist" and "knock" it against your forehead, with a pained facial expression and lips pursed, don't hit yourself too hard! Stop the "knock" an inch away from your forehead and then this sign won't hurt you a bit, but you may have to soothe someone else's hurt feelings afterward.

Taiwan

Here's another country sign, created by the Deaf in Taiwan. Using the handshape "Fist," bring your hand to the corner of your mouth and twist your wrist as if you're eating delicious sugarcane.

Handshape "5"

Handshape "5" is the manual numeric sign for the number five. Spread all the fingers out on one hand and present the palm. Remember to use strong fingers and spread them as wide as you can when you first learn this sign, to make it really clear.

Farm

Now it's time to get back to the land with your hands. "Farm" is one of the most fun signs to learn, because it is of-the-earth and extremely visual as you "till the land" across your beautiful face.

STEP 1

Position handshape "5" on the far side of your chin, with your thumb pointing toward your face. Make sure your face is visible—aim the pinky of your "5" handshape down toward the ground. Make your facial expression appropriate to the context of your sentence, and your lips should be in position to pronounce "fa" over the two steps. Your handshape "5" is a tractor's tiller that will begin farming the land in the next step!

STEP 2

Complete the sign by moving your handshape "5" across your chin to the other side of your face, with your thumb continuing to point at your chin. (This is supposed to look as if your fingers are the tines of the tractor's tiller.)

BONUS Blue Jeans

It's two, two signs in one! The sign for "blue jeans" is exactly the same as the sign for "farm." Blue jeans were invented for those who "worked the land," so the idea behind "farm" and "blue jeans" shares the same visual conceit. Your "blu" or "fa" lips position marks the difference between the signs.

Father

Raise your handshape "5" to your forehead. Position your thumb in the middle of your forehead, with the leading edge of your palm facing away from you. Tap your thumb two times against your forehead, as if you're creating a rooster's crown. Your facial expression depends on your state of mind when you're making this sign. Your lips should be in the ready-to-pronounce "fa" position.

BONUS Grandfather

Okay, so you've perfected your "father" sign. Now, using the same handshape "5," you can create the sign for "grandfather" by moving your hand away from your forehead in two outward arcs instead of tapping your thumb against your forehead twice as you did in the "father" sign.

Mother

Like "father," "mother" is a two-taps sign made with handshape "5," but instead of tapping on your forehead as you did for "father," tap on your chin twice to sign "mother." (See the "father" sequence if you need more help.)

BONUS Grandmother

Take your mother sign and move your handshape "5" away from your chin in a small arc. The instant you finish the arc, quickly repeat it a second time.

Handshape "Bent V"

If you thought handshape "Claw" was a wicked-looking sign, check out handshape "Bent V," because it's even more ruthless looking! Sometimes our students call the "Bent V" the Arthritic Claw. The description "Bent V" is based on the manual alphabet sign for the letter *V*—the universal gesture for victory. Once your hand is in the "V" position, bend your index finger and middle finger at the first two knuckles, and there you have the "Bent V" handshape.

Blind

Be careful when you form your handshape "Bent V" into the sign for "blind" because you could hurt yourself if you're not careful. Position handshape "Bent V" in front of your face and put your fingers near your eyes on each side of your nose. Then, flex those bent fingers twice. Remember, don't poke yer eye out!

Squirrel

Animal signs are always cute and fun to learn. "Squirrel" is one of our favorites, because the handshape "Bent V" and the facial expression must match perfectly or the sign won't work. This is your second two-handed sign. Make each of your hands into "Bent V" handshapes and bring both hands together under your mouth so that your middle fingers touch each other. Your facial expression is that of a hungry squirrel! Fill your cheeks with imaginary nuts and get ready to do some munching. Using your "Bent V" fingers as your razor-sharp "teeth," gnaw on an acorn by flexing your fingers in unison a few times.

Vampire

If "V" is for "victory," then "Bent V" is for "vampire!" You're the victim, and your "Bent V" is the vampire's fangs. Take your handshape "Bent V" and stab your bent-finger "fangs" into the side of your neck. Tilt your head to the side for easy blood-sucking action! Your facial expression reflects the shock and ecstasy of joining the immortal caped Prince of Darkness. If you're feeling especially ironic, you could create a "freckled vampire," even though that would be mythologically impossible, since vampires can't expose themselves to the sun to freckle.

Handshape "25"

Handshape "25" is a "lazy" handshape "5," with a quivering middle finger as the centerpiece. It takes a little bit of dexterity to pull off this handshape, but don't let that get you down if you don't get it right away. If you know advanced numbers in ASL, this handshape is the manual numeric sign for the number 25. You may need to relax your hand a bit before making this sign so that it's loose enough to flick your middle finger up and down three times fast. For the signs in this section, you won't need to flick that middle finger, but it will need to stick out more than the other fingers in order to be understood.

Lucky

There are two simple steps you'll need to cast the lady luck sign on your side, and hand-shape "25" is the key to unlocking its riches.

Step 1

Place your middle finger from your handshape "25" on your lower cheek. Your facial expression is positive, and your lips are slightly open, as if form-ing "lucky."

Step 2

Now move that middle finger from your cheek and slide it an inch or two toward your chin and then let it fly off your face. Point your middle finger outward into the empty space in front of your face so that your palm faces the person to whom you are speaking.

BONUS Fortunate

We have another synonym! If instead of say-ing "lucky" you'd prefer to say "fortunate," you can, because the sign is nearly exactly the same! The one change you'll need to make is in the form of your mouth. Change it from "lucky" to "for," and you're ready to cast your fortune upon the world.

Smart

Is it better to be lucky or is it lucky to be smart? You won't have to choose between the two when you add "smart" to your ASL arsenal.

Step 1

Take handshape "25" and put your middle finger in the center of your forehead. Your facial expression is positive and your lips are in a "sm" position.

Step 2

Now twist your handshape "25" at the wrist, away from your forehead, out into the space above your head, as if a smart idea were bursting from your brain. Your facial expression remains positive, but your lips are open and your teeth and mouth are in an "ah" position.

BONUS Bright & Intelligent

In ASL, "bright" and "intelligent" are signed just like "smart" except that the distance handshape "25" is flicked out from your forehead indicates levels of intelligence: closer is "smart," farther away is "bright," and the farthest is pure "genius."

Taste

This is a one-step sign with two taps. The reason so many of these single-step signs have taps is to show movement and repetition, since the sign is, basically, stationary. Tapping gives the receiver a quick chance for repetition and confirmation. You generally "tap" by moving the entire hand, not just a single finger. Place your handshape "25" middle finger on your chin and tap that finger (your whole hand moves) on your chin two times as if something is touching your tongue and you're tasting the flavor. Your facial expression matches what you're tasting in your sentence and your lips are in a "tay" position with your mouth open and teeth showing.

BONUS: Favor & Favorite & Type & Style

To sign both "favor" and "favorite," change your lips position to "fav"—sentence context will indicate which you mean. For "type," pronounce "ty." For "style," your lips are in a "sty" position.

Handshape "C"

Our final handshape for this chapter is the manual alphabet letter "C." When you show a "C" as a letter, make sure the edge of your palm is facing away from you, because the "C" is being read by the person watching you sign. From your perspective, handshape "C" looks backward, but it appears correctly as a "C" shape to others.

Cousin (female)

Place your handshape "C" near the bottom of your chin, and then twist it back and forth a few times a couple of inches in each direction. Your facial expression is neutral and your lips are in a "cuz" position.

BONUS Cousin (male)

In ASL, the face is divided in half by gender, with the horizontal plane of the nose being the dividing line. Many signs below the nose are female and signs above the nose are male. Location is so important in ASL because, as with the "cousin" sign, gender is dictated by the location of your handshape "C." A "cousin" near the temple is male and one near the bottom of the chin is "female."

Santa Claus

Santa Claus is coming to town on your handshape "C," and you can welcome him by creating a positive facial expression.

STEP 1

Make a handshape "C" out in front of your chin.

STEP 2

Looking big and fat and jolly, move your handshape "C" down in a small arc from your chin to your chest, suggesting Santa Claus's white beard, and you'll have created the twinkling moment of Santa Claus coming to town.

BONUS Christmas

The sign for "Christmas" is exactly the same as the sign for "Santa Claus." People will know the difference between the two signs based on the context of the sentence you create.

Sun

The glorious sign for the sun shining in the sky is created with a "suh" lips position while your eyes follow the sun into the sky above.

Step

Handshape "C" is the sun in your eye. Position your hand near the side of your face and prepare to cast off your "sun."

Step 2

In a deliberate, steady motion, move your handshape "C" sun into the sky by pushing it up on an angle into the wild blue yonder above you. After you "land" the "sun" in the sky, finish the sign with a little emphasis, as if you're plunking that burning ball of fire back in the slot where it belongs.

Manual Handshape Library

Here are all twenty-six manual handshapes in the English alphabet, for your easy reference:

A

F

K

B

G

L

C

H

M

D

I

N

E

J

O

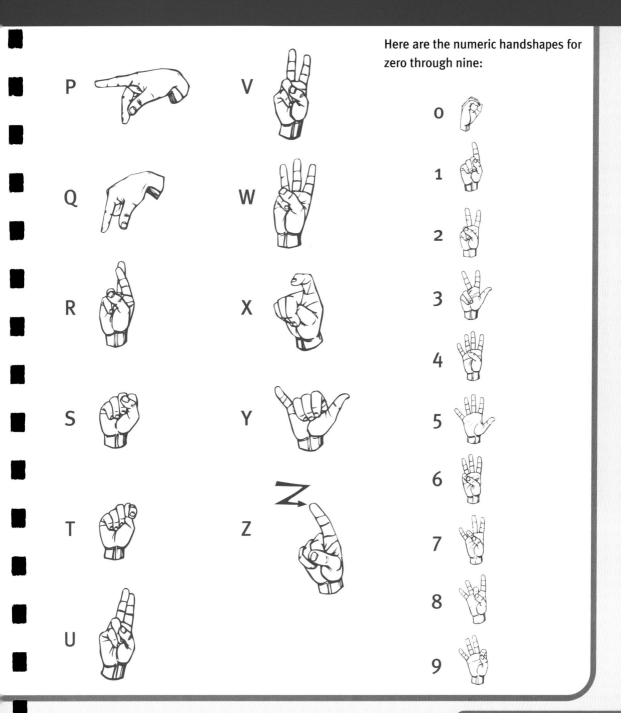

P

Q

R

S

T

U

V

W

X

Y

Z

Here are the numeric handshapes for zero through nine:

0

1

2

3

4

5

6

7

8

9

5 Check This

Ready to start throwing down the signs? Now that you've learned the basic ASL concepts, facial expressions, and handshapes, you'll be able to create all of the signs in the rest of this book. In this chapter, we start you off with some simple—and useful—words and phrases. So dig in—you'll be signin' like lightnin' in no time!

Note: The symbols that appear before each word or phrase in the following chapters show you at a glance which ASL handshape to use 🖐, what facial expression to assume 😊, how to hold your head 🙂, and how to form your lips 👄. We occasionally give you the literal ASL translation, too, if we think it will help you understand how to create the sign.

Hi

 5

 positive

 straight

 open, as if saying "ah"

Starting off friendly is always a great idea. This ASL sign is probably the same as the sign you've always used to toss a "hello," but let's break it down.

* Bring your handshape "5" up above shoulder level with your palm outward
* Move your hand sideways quickly a few times

Bye

 5

 positive or negative

 straight

 pursed "b"

Some might sign "bye" and "hi" in nearly the same way by just changing the facial expression. Not us! While much of the ASL sign for "bye" is the same as the one for "hi," we've made the following modifications just to make sure you're still with us and paying attention.

* Instead of waving your hand sideways, keep your hand steady
* Bend your fingers forward together in unison a few times
* Your facial expression depends on whether you're happy or sad to see someone leave

What's your name?

What's in a name? You can't find out unless you ask! Here's how to take the initiative in an introductory conversation.

ASL translation: (you + who?)

 1

 straight, then cocked to the side

wh-question

pursed "wh"

STEP 1 you

Take your handshape "1" and do what your mother taught you never to do: point at someone!

* Point at the person you want to reveal their name

> Pointing indicates intent and want in this case, and so, in the Deaf community, pointing is preferred to being unclear. When you level your hand to point, give the point a little extra emphasis in the direction of the person.

STEP 2 who?

* Lift your pointing handshape "1" to your chin
* Extend your thumb to touch your chin as you turn your head slightly
* Furrow your eyebrows
* Bend your index finger quickly twice, as if pulling the trigger on a gun
* Lower your hand, keep eye contact steady, and wait for your answer

My name is _____

Knowing how to identify yourself if you're asked the question you just learned is another fine way to carry on an introductory conversation with a Deaf person. You can either finger spell your name to fill in the blank or, if you have Deaf friends, they can provide you with a sign name. We'll use Janna's sign name in this example, since we discussed it in Chapter 1.

ASL translation: (j + my + name)

 J, Flat B, and H   positive

 straight   pursed "m"

STEP ❶ j

Janna's sign name begins on the opposite shoulder from her manual alphabet letter "J" hand. You can just finger spell your name for this step.

✳ Use your pinky finger to draw a "J" in the air

STEP ❷ my

✳ Place a handshape "Flat B" on your chest, indicating "my"

Step ③ name

The sign for "name" is the manual alphabet handshape "H," and while this is a new handshape, it's easy to create.

* Make both hands into the universal shape for a gun (add the middle fingers of both hands to help form the barrel of the gun with your index fingers)

* Swiftly "tap" one gun barrel against the top of the second gun barrel

What's up?

You'll see this sign used all the time—sometimes even pronounced "wassup?"—and many times it's used as the preferred greeting to "hi." This sign can also be signed with only one hand when you're comfortable and relaxed, and the person you're talking to is as relaxed and laid back as you are.

 25

tilted back a bit and to the side

 wh-question

 pursed "wh"

STEP **1**

* Place handshape "25" middle fingers of both hands on the center of your chest
* Tilt your head slightly up, eyebrows down, shoulders forward just a bit

STEP **2**

* Take your handshape "25" hands and quickly "flick" both hands up from your chest and into the air in front of you in a straight line in line with your shoulders
* Your facial expression is anticipatory
* Hunch forward, waiting for the answer to your question

Yes

You'll use the "yes" sign a lot. You can use it to agree, to show understanding, or to show that you're down with the ideas being expressed. You're nodding your head in agreement when you use this sign.

 Fist positive

 straight, but nodding up and down "ye"

* Raise your handshape "Fist" in front of you, with your thumb facing the viewer

* "Nod" your handshape "Fist" twice at the wrist

* Smile if you're happy

* Always raise your eyebrows with this sign

* Nod your head along with your hand

No

If you use "yes" a lot, you'll use "no" even more when you first start out learning ASL, because you won't understand what's going on around you. Shake your head and sign "no" to let people know that you aren't getting it. You can say "no" to questions or ideas or to mimed indicators. Using the sign in addition to shaking your head will leave no doubt as to where you stand in your understanding.

 modified N

 shaking side to side

 negative

 pursed "n"

Sometimes you'll see "no" signed aggressively, right in your face, with a single hard tap. You can say "no" in a variety of ways, like signing it ten times in a row to make a point—that you're not interested in what's being asked.

* Make a modified "N" handshape—tap your index and middle fingers down in unison twice on your thumb
* Your eyebrows are down

Why?

You'll see "why" a lot when you first start hanging out with the Deaf because Deaf people like to know reasons for behavior and beliefs. Get ready to sign this and to answer it when you see it flying.

 25

cocked to the side

 wh-question

 pursed "wh"

* Hunch your shoulders forward
* Bring your head forward a bit
* Eyebrows are down
* Bring handshape "25" up to shoulder height and position your middle finger near your temple, as if making a psychic connection with your brain
* Pull the wondering out of your mind with your middle finger as it quivers twice to make the "why" sign

Thank you

Someone who gives you something or who pleases you deserves a "thank you."

 signer's choice—Flat B or B

 straight

 positive

 "th" pronunciation

STEP 1

You can use either handshape "Flat B" or handshape "B" to make this sign. The choice is yours. You'll see both handshapes used in the Deaf community. Use whichever is most comfortable for you. We'll use "Flat B" for this demonstration.

* Bring the tips of your handshape "Flat B" fingers under your chin and smile

STEP 2

Now here's where this sign gets slightly tricky.

* Move your handshape "Flat B" away from your body a foot or so, by moving your hand up slightly, away, then down making a small arc.

You're making the tiniest of arcs; you need that arc because if you simply move your "Flat B" in a straight line, you're saying "good."

Good

Yes, the only difference between signing "thank you" and "good" in ASL is that tiny little arc. You must be careful here to make it clear which sign you mean. If you're using this sign in a sentence, then context will help the viewer understand your meaning, but if you're using the sign alone or as an interjection, then you need to make clear movements. Here's how a few things change from saying "thank you" to "good."

 Flat B   positive   pursed "g"

∗ Using the same handshape "Flat B" setup, space, and area you used for saying "thank you," modify the movement straight down from your mouth to the space in front of your body

Sometimes you'll see the Deaf use a second hand in handshape "Flat B" to "stop the hand falling," with a little backhanded clap at the end of the sign to give it emphasis. The street way to sign "good" is to use one hand and stop the sign with determination.

Choice Word) WHAT

This sign for "what" is used in context here as an indicator for explanation, like "What pets do you have?" or "What's your astrological sign?" This isn't the sign you use for "what" in the Hearing-world context when you didn't hear what someone said, and say "What?" as a prompt for them to repeat it for you.

 Claw   wh-question

 cocked back, up, and to the side   pursed "wh"

*   Turn your handshape "Claw" upward so that both palms are facing the sky

*   Your arms and fingers are firm and precise! Pretend you're carrying a heavy rock in each hand, to help give your arms weight

*   The tips of your fingers should be around the height of your shoulders

*   Quickly quiver your hands back and forth an inch or two in each direction

6 Step Off!

Remember earlier when we warned you this book wasn't your mother's ASL? You're about to find out why. Now we're gonna get down and dirty. Don't let your mother know you know these signs, or she'll wash your hands out with soap!

Fuck you/Fuck him/Fuck her/Fuck them/Fuck off/Fuck it

You know the words. We'll give you the context. You already know the sign. Just be careful where and how you practice it, because the unintended result of making this sign with the wrong person could result in bodily harm.

duh!

your choice

your choice

sneering "f"

Fuck you

We prefer the fuck you handshape that uses three fingers bent at the second knuckle with a rigidly extended middle finger. When you're saying "fuck you" to one person, you make the handshape and then thrust the back of your hand in their direction with great force. That's a "fuck you" with Deaf attitude, and a visualization they will not soon forget.

Fuck him/her

If you want to say "fuck" to a person other than the one you're speaking to, then change the direction of your handshape to land in the place where that person is located, either in the room, in the space you've created in the context of your sentence, or, if they're dead in hell, toward the ground. Remember to make the sign sharp and emphatic for best effect.

Fuck them

This can be an effective "fuck" that can lend itself to a wide swath of humanity and associates. You can "fuck them" individually by rapidly thrusting the handshape in the direction of each of those on your "fuck" list, or you can make one thrust and then kind of arc your hand all around and up and down and sideways until you've given the sign to everyone on your shit list.

Fuck off

This sign is slightly different from a straight "fuck." This sign tells people that you want to be left alone in the most direct way. Direct this sign to the person you want to get rid of and, at the peak of the "fuck" thrust, quickly bring all your fingers into your palm, shoot your thumb up, and move your hand away from your body like a baseball umpire calling someone out at the plate; that "Yer out!" part of the sentence is the "off" part of the "fuck off" sign.

Fuck it

The "fuck it" sign requires more of a dejected, "I give up" delivery that brings pity on the person signing the sentence. Take the "fuck you" handshape and turn the hand downward, then stab your finger downward with less relish than you would with a regular "fuck," because this "fuck it" is like throwing your hat on the floor with disgust.

Choice Word) THE MIDDLE FINGER

The "fuck" signs you've learned here that deal with giving someone your middle finger have nothing to do with intercourse. These "fucks" are merely insults and "back at ya" verbs. The signs for sexual fucking are more explicit and even more varied. We'll get to those a bit later, in Chapter 11.

Shit

Everybody loves "shit!" "Shit" is the all-time, No. 1 asked-for sign from our students, and, like "fuck" before, there are many ways in which the Deaf sign "shit," but we'll give you our favorite. "Shit" is also your first double-fisted sign—you'll use a different handshape for each hand to make this sign.

ASL translation: (food + hit + colon)

 5 and Fist   negative

 straight   "sh" pronunciation

 STEP **1** food + hit    STEP **2** hit + colon

* Spread one hand into a wide-span handshape "5"
* Raise it to shoulder level while aiming your thumb downward
* Make the handshape "Fist" with your other hand and position it at waist level, with your thumb and index finger facing up toward the downward thumb of your other hand

* Plunge your handshape "5" thumb into the natural "hole" created by your thumb and index finger in your handshape "Fist"
* When your thumb sticks in your fist, "throb" your "Fist" fingers for a second, as if food were hitting your colon

Bullshit

You may see this sign made with a handshape "B" and a handshape "S" from the manual sign language alphabet, but we prefer a more ASL approach.

 modified B

sideways

 negative

"boo"

* Modify handshape "B" by folding your middle finger and ring finger into your palm and holding them there with your thumb—you've now created a bull with horns
* Twist to the side, get the "head" of the bull in line with your shoulder, and deliver the sign with your best "fuck you" hard thrust in the direction of the person you're calling out

Asshole

This is another sign that uses different handshapes on each hand. There are lots of signs for "asshole," but our favorite one to teach could also be mistaken for the universal sign for "rimming" in the gay community. If you don't know what "rimming" means, we aren't going to tell you here!

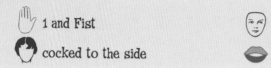

1 and Fist

cocked to the side

negative

"ah"

* Place one hand in a handshape "Fist" near your chest
* Open up the fist a little bit so that you can see through the hole in your loosened fist (you can also just use manual alphabet handshape "O," if you like)
* Take your other hand, form it into handshape "1," and place the tip of your index finger in the rim of the hole in the fist you created with your other hand
* Slowly circle your finger around the rim of the hole— keep it on the rim because if that finger slips deeper inside your fist, you're creating a whole other sign that we haven't gotten to yet

Dick

The sign for "dick" is the same as the sign for "penis" and "cock," and since they're all signed in exactly the same way, we don't feel we can quite call the extras bonus signs, but, if we had the poor taste to go for the cheap joke, we wouldn't hesitate to call them boner signs.

P

straight

negative

"dee"

* Tap the "bottom" of the "P" (your middle finger) on the tip of your nose twice—that's the sign for "dick," "penis," and "cock" all in the same stroke

The manual alphabet "P" handshape is one you may not recognize, but you can create it by using handshape "1" and releasing your middle finger so that you're making the universal "peace" sign, then simply twist your hand in toward your face—your hand will naturally change into the "P" handshape.

Bitch

This sign is the noun, not the verb.

 B

 negative

 straight

 pursed "b"

* Take your handshape "B" and tap your chin one time with the leading edge of your index finger

That's it. That's the sign. It's crisp and clean and done only once. Make sure you're looking at the right person when you sign "bitch," because if your eyes stray around the room, you might inadvertently insult someone. This sign is well known throughout the Deaf community.

BONUS Bastard

In Chapter 4, we discussed how the face is divided in half by gender. Most female indicators are made on the face below the nose, while the male signs are performed above the horizontal line of the nose. Well, if you want to sign "bastard," you use exactly the same setup you used for "bitch," except instead of tapping your chin once, you tap your handshape "B" in the center of your forehead once. Be careful with handshape position, because if you happen to turn your handshape "B" palm outward so that your palm is facing the world and the back of your hand taps your forehead, you'll be signing "fireman" instead of "bastard." If you're feeling daring and you aren't near a firehouse or in sight of a hard-working fireman, practice signing "bastard" and "fireman," so that you can see and feel the difference. While you're doing that, realize that your signing practice could be interpreted as "bastard fireman."

What a loser!

When you say the sentence "What a loser," you'll combine two different handshapes in one hand, in two steps. It'll be easy to sign, and your superior attitude will add just the right punch to the insult.

ASL translation: (no + good + you)

 N and G

 aristocratic and tilted back

 negative

 pursed "n"

Step ❶ no

Step ❷ good + you

✳ Purse those lips and create the manual alphabet handshape for "N" mid-torso

✳ Add tension to your arm as you form the handshape, so it'll give the right amount of spring for step two

Practice this sign and you'll see how it looks like a magic trick as your hand flashes from "N" to "G." It's that very flippant move that gives the sign its power and street cred.

✳ With the energy in your handshape "N" (no) hand ready to burst from your fingers, twist your wrist outward with a kind of "flip" action and, during that critical flip, change your hand-shape "N" to handshape "G" (good) by the time your hand comes to a rest

✳ Point your "G" in the direction of the person you're banging with the sign

When was the last time you bathed?

This is our first lengthy sign, so we'll cut it up in four chunks to help you get the idea of how the translation is done from English to ASL. Be sure to make each step singular and important in your judgment that's disguised as a question.

ASL translation: (power + stink! + bath + need)

 Claw. First. F, A, and X   negative, wh-question

 varies with each step   open-mouthed

STEP ❶ power

* Show your muscle by creating a hand-shape "Fist"
* Take your other hand in handshape "Claw," silently mouth "cha," and make a big, dramatic move of showing the powerful size of your muscle

STEP ❷ stink!

The next step is the universal sign for "stink," and we're sure you know how to make a face as if you're smelling a cheese fart at midnight, as you pinch your nose in disgust.

* Pinch your nose

For the ASL record, that nose-pinch is made with manual alphabet handshape "F" twisted around to clamp on to your nose, in case you're keeping a record of these things.

Step ③ bath

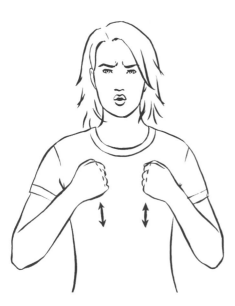

* Form both hands into handshape "A"
* Place them both knuckles-down on your chest
* Swiftly move your hands up and down your chest a few times, as if you're taking a bath

Step ④ need

The final step is to show "need." Express it using the manual alphabet handshape "X" (also a modified handshape "Bent V," minus your middle finger).

* Close your hand into a fist
* Stick out your index finger and bend it down at the second knuckle
* Move your entire hand up and down twice in front of you

Tough luck

Our students love this sign. Once they learn it, they use it on us, their friends, their pets, strangers on the street...

ASL translation: (too + bad)

 T and B

 cocky

 negative

 "too"

STEP **1** too

This sign uses the same magical movement you previously learned in the "What a loser" sentence.

STEP **2** bad

* Make manual alphabet handshape "T" and cock your hand shoulder-high

* Then, with tension coiling in your arm, "fling" the handshape "T" away from your body

* As your hand is moving, quickly change that "T" into a handshape "B" before you stop the sign a few inches away from where you began

The trick to getting this sign to work well is the speed and snappiness of the transition from handshape "T" to "B," so you'll need practice to make it perfect. Once you've got the magic down, try it out on a few people! You throw the "T" to "B" snap in the direction of the one you're dissing.

7 Eat It!

Going out to feed that angry, growling monster in the pit of your belly can be an event fraught with delays and disasters. These sentences will help you get what you want when you need it, and help you fight back if you're stuck in a Hell's Kitchen from which you cannot escape.

Man, I'm starving!

This sign is especially animated, and if you perform the facial expression properly, you could get your message across without even having to move your arms. The key to this sentence is to really show in your face your strong desire to eat.

ASL translation: (wow + me + hungry!)

 Claw, 1, and C
 straight

 hungry!
 pursed "ooo"

STEP ❶ wow

* Raise handshape "Claw" to the side of your head
* Move it back and forth on the ear-to-eye plane five inches in each direction in a syncopated "throbbing" manner, as if you have a headache

> This "wow" sign also means "Man!" (as an interjection, not as a gender description), "Oh boy!" and "Oh goodness!"

STEP ❷ me

* Point at yourself midchest with hand-shape "1," indicating "me"

The sign for "hungry" and "starving" is made with handshape "C" drawn down the center of the chest. This sign is used to indicate an internal craving for food; it's not, however, the same as the sign you'd use to show sexual hunger or the lust you might have for a person. To use this sign to say something like "I'm hungry for sex" wouldn't be understood. Lust and desire will be covered in full in Chapter 11.

STEP **3** hungry

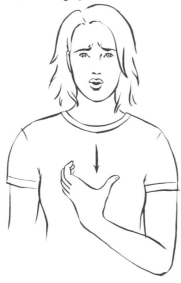

* Place handshape "C" on the middle of your chest
* Make sure the open end of the "C" is facing up toward your neck
* Dramatically drag handshape "C" down your chest a few inches, to indicate how "hungry" you are

Make sure your face is showing your desperate hunger—that's how to emphasize the exclamation point at the end of the sentence!

Did you make reservations?

This question can help you get to the bottom of confusion in a restaurant or when plans are being made for a hot night out on the town.

ASL translation: (save + finish?)

 V and 5

straight

 yes/no question, eyebrows up

 "f" shape

STEP ❶ save

This movement means "save," "reserve," or "keep" (as in "keep it safe," not "keep this thing").

* Make one hand into handshape "5" and place it two inches in front of your chest
* Form the manual alphabet handshape "V" with your other hand (straighten out the two fingers in the handshape "Bent V" you've already learned)
* Tap that handshape "V" twice on the back of your handshape "5" hand

STEP ❷ finish

This is the first half of the word "finish."

* Create handshape "5" with both hands and raise eyebrows to indicate you're asking a question
* Raise hands to shoulder level, with the back of your palms facing the person watching you

STEP **3**

* Finish "finish" by twisting both hand-shape "5" wrists in toward each other and downward a few inches

You can use one hand for "finish" if you want.

Where's our waiter?

Wondering where your waiter went at dinner can get frustrating. Here's how to pose the inquiry to get an immediate answer.

ASL translation: (waiter + where?)

 Bullshit (modified B) and 1

 curious, slightly cocked to the side

 wh-question, eyebrows down

 pursed "wh"

STEP ❶ waiter

* Make the "Bullshit" handshape from Chapter 6, but this time, turn your wrist 180 degrees so that the "Bullshit" sign is reversed

With the back of your "Bullshit" hand facing you at shoulder level, what used to be the tips of a bull's horns have now become two fingers on which your waiter balances a tray. Once you make this "waiter" sign—it has no movement— move on to the next step.

STEP ❷ where

* Change your hand from the "Bullshit" handshape to hand-shape "1" and move it back and forth three inches on a horizontal plane to ask "Where?"

* Your eyebrows are down and your head and shoulders slightly forward, in anticipation of an answer

Thirsty

Now that you've got the waiter's attention, you want to let him know you're a bit thirsty. Here's how to indicate that your thirst needs quenching.

ASL translation: (thirsty)

 1

tilted back

 negative

"thir"

The slower you move your finger and the more desperate you make your facial expression, the thirstier you are, so always keep speed, movement, and facial expression in mind. This sign for "thirsty" is also the sign for "sexual lust," so be careful how you use this sign, lest people think you want the wrong kind of thirst quenched.

* With your head tilted back and to the side, place the index finger of your handshape "1" against the side of your exposed throat right below the chin line
* Slowly drag your finger down your neck until you reach your collarbone

Can I get a menu?

When you have a hankerin' for more than a hunk o' cheese, you're gonna need to know what else is available. Here's how to place your first, and most important, order: getting a menu.

ASL translation: (list + food + have?)

 Flat B, Flat O, and Bent B

 location specific

 yes/no question

 pursed circular and pursed flat

STEP ❶ list

Menus consist of elements lined up in list form, so one hand becomes the menu while your other hand lists the food choices.

* Make one hand into handshape "Flat B"
* Create handshape "Bent B" with the other
* Using the edge of your "Bent B" hand, identify each item on the menu
* Inch down your "Flat B" palm, lifting and lowering your "Bent B" handshape as you go

STEP ❷ food

* Make one hand into handshape "Flat O"
* Bring your fingertips to your chin, tapping twice to indicate "food"
* Purse your lips in a "foo" position to suggest both the word "food" and the act of eating what you're holding in your "Flat O" handshape

STEP ❸ have

You may see "have" signed with both hands
in handshape "Bent B," and that's fine and
totally proper and correct, but it isn't street.
So just use a single hand for "have" and, if
you want to be really fluent, use the same
hand to sign "food" in step two and "have" in
this step and link them together in one fluid
movement for greatest effect. You'll also
notice that your thumb sticks up, out of
"proper" handshape "B" position—that's
okay because that's physiology at work. You
can't sign "have" and not have your thumb
stick straight up in the air! Try it, and you'll
see what we mean.

* Bring the fingertips of a handshape "Bent
  B" against the top of your chest on the
  same side to suggest "have"

* Lean forward a bit in anticipation and shrug
  your shoulders forward, waiting for a reply

Gross, I found a bug in my soup, take it back!

ASL translation:
(bowl + soup + bug + there + disgust + bowl-there + back-to-you)

 A, modified H, Bent B, Bent V, 1, and Claw   negative

 straight   pursed

STEP ❶ bowl

First you need to place the bowl of soup in time and space.

* Make two "C" handshapes
* Place them in the space in front of your body
* Using a swooping motion, define the sides and size of the soup bowl by arcing each handshape "C" up and out to the side

> This motion looks as if you're smoothing the sides of a clay pot on a potters' wheel.

STEP ❷ soup

* Dig into your soup with a modified handshape "H" in the shape of a spoon (bend the index finger and the middle finger forward into a scoop shape)
* Your other hand is in the handshape "Bent B" position, with the palm facing the sky (this is the bowl)
* Dip handshape "H" into your handshape "Bent B" bowl a few times, bringing your "soup" up to your mouth each time
* Your facial expression is excited and hungry
* Eyebrows are up

> "Bent B" is handshape "Flat B" with your fingers folded down perpendicular to your palm.

Step ❸ bug

Eew! (You gotta make your facial expression jump to show the "Eew!" interjection.) You just found a bug in your soup! It's important in this step that you indicate with your alarmed facial expression that something odd has happened.

* Using handshape "Bent V," raise it in front of your face so your wrist touches the tip of your nose and the "trigger" fingers stick straight out from your nose
* Squeeze the fingers of your handshape "Bent V" twice, as if you're pulling the trigger on a gun, to indicate the antennae of the bug moving around in space
* Your facial expression should twitch along with the triggering of your antennae

Step ❹ there

You have to set the location of the bug in your soup.

* Create "there" with handshape "1"
* Point straight down into where you created your soup in step one
* Your facial expression must be disgusted, nauseous, ready to hurl
* Your eyes stare down at the soup to direct those watching your conversation to the right location

STEP **5** disgust

* Create handshape "Claw"—remember to keep your fingers firm
* Center it on your abdomen, and then churn it in circles on your stomach three times
* Your facial expression is sick
* Tongue is out
* Your eyes are drooping as you try not to imagine what part of the bug you just ate

STEP **6** bowl-there

It's important that you quickly reestablish the original location of the "bowl-there" to cement the next step.

* Use handshape "C" on both hands, as in step one, as if your hands are actually holding the sides of the bowl

STEP **7** back-to-you

* Pick up the "bowl" between your handshape "C" hands
* Throw it back in your waiter's face by thrusting your hands straight away from your body at an upward angle until your arms are fully extended and your palms are facing away from you

It's all in the tonguing

You've been actively using your tongue since Chapter 2. Continue to use it in this chapter and beyond. Your tongue is invaluable in ASL because you use your tongue to show negativity, like "not yet" or "didn't do it," and emotions, like "disgust," "strong dislike," "never seen before," and even actions, like "throw up," "taste," and "take a pill."

Gross, I found a bug in my soup, take it back!

STEP **1**

STEP **2**

STEP **3**

STEP **4**

STEP **5**

STEP **6**

STEP **7**

Yum

To convey the idea of "yummy" or "delicious," start with a modified handshape "25," in which your middle finger and thumb come together to form a circle (this is also the "8" handshape).

ASL translation: (delicious)

 modified 25 (numerical handshape 8)   positive

 slightly tilted back   slightly open "dee" pronunciation

Step ❶

❋ Bring the handshape close to your lips as you smile, brighten your eyes, and raise your eyebrows

Step ❷

❋ In a quick movement, take that same modified handshape "25" and "snap" your index finger down on your thumb as you pull your hand away from your mouth six inches or so

The finger-snap movement might take you a little bit of practice to perfect. The movement of this "delicious" sign suggests the landing of food on your tongue, and your taste buds "snapping" to attention with oral delight!

This food sucks!

So you made your reservation and now the food is terrible! Here's how to visually express your disgust.

ASL translation: (food + disgust)

 5 and Flat O

 back, then forward

 negative

 pursed, then open

STEP ❶ food

* Bring all your fingers and thumbs together to form the beak of a bird—handshape "Flat O"
* Tap that beak handshape "Flat O" twice on your chin
* Stick out your tongue in a big way

STEP ❷ disgust

* Your handshape "Flat O" beak changes into handshape "5"
* With your thumb pointing near your mouth and your palm facing the person you're telling, wrinkle up your nose
* Furrow your brow
* Stick that tongue out even further

S<small>TEP</small> **3**

You've successfully shown what you think of the food as it now pools in an undigested pile of puke at your feet. Students love to use this "disgust" and "vomit" and "really hate" sign in lots of different one-sign contexts: "This test is disgusting." "Your dress makes me vomit." "This is what I think of your new girlfriend."

* Quickly move handshape "5" in an arc down and away from your face

I need a stiff drink!

You've had a hard day and you're looking for some liquid relaxation. Find a bartender and let this phrase fly!

ASL translation: (drink [alcohol] + strong + need)

 Single C, Fist, and X   desperate

 straight    pursed, then exposed teeth

STEP ❶ drink

Handshape "Single C" (just the index finger and thumb make the "C" shape, as opposed to the whole hand as in the regular "C" handshape) is used for describing mixed drinks with alcohol, while the regular manual alphabet handshape "C" is the generic sign for drinking whatever else. You can remember the difference more easily if you imagine your mixed drink in a small glass tumbler held delicately between thumb and index finger. An extra-large soda will be in a giant tub of a cup that'll take your entire hand to heft to your parched lips.

* Using handshape "Single C," raise your drink to your mouth, elbow angled out away from your face
* Tip the glass at your wrist to indicate a one-swig motion that tosses the liquid into your mouth

STEP ❷ strong

* Take your handshape "Fist" and, with knuckles facing away from you, bring that hand up to eye level about a foot away from your face
* Tense up your arm a few times so your muscles twitch and jitter to indicate the strong power of the stiff drink you want to imbibe

Step **3** need

It's time for your desperation to show.
Sign "need" using handshape "X."

✳ "Nod" your entire hand at the wrist twice in front of you at chest level

Your facial expression is the key here—you need to show those teeth to help express your brazen desire! You should also practice smoothly transitioning between your "strong" and "need" handshapes. You don't have to move your arm, just change handshape "Fist" to handshape "X" in a fluid motion.

8 The Fam and Your Peeps

Up to this point, you've had a bit of an introduction to signs, context, handshapes, facial expressions, and movement. In this chapter, you'll begin to lengthen your ASL sentences to more fully express larger ideas. We've broken these sentences up into lots of separate steps to make it easier.

I can't stand my in-laws!

If you love your in-laws, you already know how to sign that: blow them a kiss. If, however, you are like many normal people struggling in the whirlwind of mixing families, you may not appreciate everything about your in-laws. This little sentence will assist you in releasing some steam while also serving as a call for help to those in the know.

ASL translation: (parents + in-law + bear-with + no)

 5, Flat B, L, and A

 straight, then cocked

 negative

 pursed "no"

STEP ❶ mother

Remember the "mother" sign you learned in Chapter 4? Use it here. (See p. 100.)

* Take handshape "5"
* Stick thumb on chin
* Don't tap

STEP ❷ father

Next, use the sign for "father" you also learned back in Chapter 4. (See p. 100.)

* Take the same handshape "5" you used in step one
* Move it up to your forehead to indicate "father"

STEPS ❸ & ❹ in-law

This sign is the "I" in "law" being placed on an open law book. This "in-law" step modifies the "mother" and "father" signs. Since you signed "mother" and "father" first before making this sign, in the ASL sequence you're indicating that the mother and father are bound to you by law, not by blood.

* Place handshape "Flat B" near your head as if you're showing the page of a book, with your palm serving as the open page

* Place a handshape "L" near the top of your open palm

* To finish "in-law," keep everything the same as in step three, but lift your "L" handshape and drop it down a few inches to reset it on the base of your handshape "Flat B" palm

The "L" handshape is made as if you're making a gun with your hand: index finger out as the barrel, thumb straight up as the hammer, and the rest of your fingers folded into your palm as the handle of the gun.

STEP ⑤ bear-with

* Purse your lips
* Make your shoulders really tight
* Take the tip of your handshape "A" thumb and touch it to your top lip
* Drag that thumbnail straight down across your mouth until it reaches your chin to indicate "bear with"

If you draw blood during this sign, that's okay, because you'll be letting the world know just how you really feel about your in-laws. If, however, you have a facial expression that is positive and you drag your thumb down your chin twice in quick succession, that means you're "patient" and not trying to just "bear with."

STEP ⑥ no

You just made the sign for "bear with," but even with your negative facial expression (and possible bloodletting), you haven't yet modified the sentence to indicate that you have no patience for the in-laws you don't like. To make sure you sign "no" to modify "bear with," you need to add even more negative attitude.

* Screw up your face into a mean frown
* Clearly shake your head "no" a couple of times to punctuate your negative feelings

This sentence is hardcore ASL—you won't see this kind of basic-instinct sentence in regular ASL books.

I can't stand my in-laws!

Step **3**

Step **4**

Step **5**

Step **6**

My brother is a whiner.

Everyone's entitled to a little whine with dinner once in a while, but not all the time! Use this sign to say how much your brother bothers you with his nagging and silly complaints. We'll also tell you how to modify this sign from "brother" to "sister."

My brother is a whiner.

ASL translation: (brother + complain + too much)

 L, C, and Bent B   negative

 straight   pursed "bro" or "sis"

STEP ❶ brother

* Put both hands in "L" handshapes to create "brother"
* Position one hand with the tip of your thumb touching the side of your forehead
* Place the second hand in front of you at the waistline

To make this sentence about your "sister" instead of your "brother," just move the handshape "L" down from your temple to the side of your chin.

STEP ❷

* Drop the top handshape "L" down to rest on top of the other handshape "L" at your waist
* Cock your thumb on the upper hand-shape so it looks as if you're about to shoot a gun

That cocked thumb indicates that you aren't pointing at something but rather establishing a relationship with the person you defined on your face. If you're talking about "sister" instead, this sign stays exactly the same.

Step 3 complain

* Create handshape "C"
* Tap the open part of the "C" on your chest a few times to indicate "whining," "complaining," and "bitching"
* Your face should be reflecting the face your brother or sister uses while in the whining mode

Step 4 too much

* Using "Bent B" on both hands, place one hand atop the other in front of your chest to begin the sign for "too much" or "in excess" or "way more"

STEP **5**

✳ Lift the "Bent B" handshape that is resting on top straight up to head level

The height you choose indicates the degree of the whine factor. Some students reach as high as they can and then rise onto their tiptoes to show that the whining is beyond their ability to fully and physically describe while standing on two feet. That kind of exaggerated signing style is enjoyed and welcomed in the Deaf community.

My brother is a whiner.

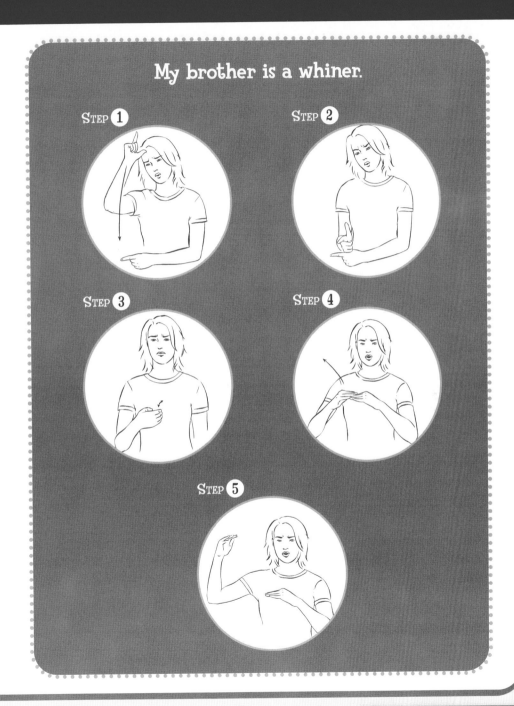

STEP 1

STEP 2

STEP 3

STEP 4

STEP 5

Mom's drunk again.

In an effort to achieve gender equality, we'll dis Mom in this sentence, though, like "brother" in the sentence before, you can swap out "mom" for "father" (or even "grandmother" or "grandfather," or "monster" or "vampire").

ASL translation: (mom + drunk + again)

 5, A, Bent B, and Flat B

 disgusted (or happy, if you're the one who got her drunk!)

 straight

 pursed "dra"

STEP ❶ mom

※ Use handshape "5" to create the "mom" sign by tapping the tip of your thumb against your chin twice

STEP ❷

※ Make handshape "A" a foot in front of your face (the tip of your thumb should be pointing toward your face)

STEP ❸ drunk

- ✳ Using handshape "A," create an arc across the front of your body from your chin down to your chest on the opposite side of your body

- ✳ While you're drawing that arc for "drunk," wobble your head back and forth a bit to suggest the drunken state you're describing

STEP ❹

- ✳ Make handshape "Bent B" on one hand out to the side of your body with the palm facing the space in front of your torso

- ✳ With your other hand, make a "landing strip" with a handshape "Flat B" near your hip with that palm facing the sky

STEP 5 again

* Move your handshape "Bent B" in an arc through the air
* The tips of your fingers land in the middle of your outstretched handshape "Flat B" palm
* Your facial expression is puckered — disgusted by your pickled mother

Mom's drunk again.

STEP 1

STEP 2

STEP 3

STEP 4

STEP 5

I'm gonna hang with the boys tonight.

This is a sentence that's got a lot of tapping and large movements. Be deliberate in your motions. There's no rush to hurry through the steps. We don't modify "boys" in this sentence because gender doesn't matter in this instance—the group you're referring to is already known and familiar based on the context of the conversation you're having.

I'm gonna hang with the boys tonight.

ASL translation: (tonight + friends + group-go-to + hang out)

 Flat B, Bent B, 1, C, and 25

 varies based on sign location

 neutral

 tight, flat

STEP ❶ tonight

* Place both hands in a handshape "Bent B" position
* Cross both hands to meet in front of your body with both palms down
* Tap the top "Bent B" on top of the other "Bent B" twice to indicate "tonight"

STEP ❷ friends

* Making handshape "1" with both hands, bring them together in the space in front of your body and hook each index finger onto the other one at the first knuckle
* Quickly press each finger against the other...

Step ❸

* ...then release the hooked index fingers and reverse your handshape "1" positions by twisting your hands at the wrists in opposite directions
* Quickly repeat the hooking action you just did in step two

This means "friends," in which each finger represents a person, and you hook them together in hugging, buddy-buddy, best-friends-forever, modified-"pinky-swear" fashion.

Step ❹ group-go-to

This step is a little tricky. To sign "group-go-to," you must first create one location in order to show another, separate location where the group "goes to" in space. If you decide the place you're going to is on your left side, and you refer to that location again later on in the conversation, you must keep that initial location intact in the space you created by returning to it or pointing to it, so the person you're talking to will understand that you mean the same place in space.

* Create your initial space by making both hands into handshape "C"
* Have the open part of each hand face the other (that space between your two handshape "C" hands indicates the group, not the space)

STEP ⑤

STEP ⑥ hang out

To start "hanging out," you need to create handshape "25" with both hands, but don't move the middle fingers.

* Take that "group" you created in step four and slowly move it to the new location where the group will "go-to" to hang out together

* Keep your hands at the same distance away from each other so that the size of your group doesn't shrink or grow

* Place one handshape "25" in the space in front of you at head level with the palm facing slightly down, and the other hand at shoulder level with the palm facing the sky

As you think about this step in the sentence, try to picture the size of your group in your hands. If your group is three people, your hands will indicate a smaller "group-go-to," and if you have twenty-two people, your hands need to indicate that larger "group-go-to" size.

STEP 7

Each middle finger represents people "hanging out."

* Make a series of simultaneous small circles with each handshape "25" on a horizontal plane while moving each hand diagonally across your body from high to low, without changing the physical space between your two fingers

STEP 8

* End the sign in front of the opposite shoulder from where you began

I'm gonna hang with the boys tonight.

STEP **1**

STEP **2**

STEP **3**

STEP **4**

STEP **5**

STEP **6**

STEP **7**

STEP **8**

Bring a six-pack—actually, bring a case!

This sentence is the longest in this chapter. We break it down into eight easy steps, but it's probably best to learn this sign sober, not after downing the case!

Bring a six-pack—actually, bring a case!

ASL translation: (beer + [rectangle shape] + bring-here + oh! + "cha!")

 Flat B, B, and 5

 straight

 feel the "cha!"

 pursed "b" and open "cha"

Step **1** beer

* Make a handshape "B" with your palm facing your audience
* Place your hand on the side of your head
* Drag the handshape down the side of your face two times to indicate "beer"

Step **2**

Now we need to create the six-pack by suggesting its outline.

* Make handshape "Flat B" with both hands
* Bring your hands to either side of your chest with the palms facing each other

You've created two sides of the six-pack. Now you have to create the other two sides so everyone will know you're talking about a six-pack.

Your hands are not as far apart as they were in step two, because a six-pack is not a square, it's a rectangle.

Step 3

Step 4 bring-here

The sign for "bring" uses the same handshape "Flat B."

* Use your same "Flat B" handshapes and move them parallel to each other about a foot apart in front of you, with the palms facing your chest

* Create the "six-pack" sign quickly by combining the signs in steps two and three without hesitation, as if you're using a cookie cutter

* With both palms facing the sky, put one hand higher than the other, then move your hands as a unit, as if you're bringing the six-pack of beer into the center space

STEP **5**

* Bring both hands, palms up, in front of your body as the conclusion to the "bring" sign started in step four, and pause for a moment as you hold the six-pack before you

* Your facial expression should be tentative, because you're about to change your mind

STEP **6** oh!

But wait, you've changed your mind! (You must sell that change of plan with your facial expression for this part of the sentence to work.) You don't want a six-pack, you want an entire case instead!

* Hold handshape "5" up to your audience with the palm facing out to indicate a stop

* Shake your hand back and forth along with your head as if you're erasing what you're saying

* Your positive facial expression is "Oh wait! I have a better idea!"

STEP 7

STEP 8 cha!

* Create the same sign with handshape "Flat B" as you did in step two, but make the space between your hands larger to suggest a case of beer, not a six-pack

* Silently mouth "cha!" with your open mouth as you create the same hand-shape "Flat B" as described above in step three, but make this final "dimension" sign really big in comparison with step three, because you want everyone to know that you want a *case* of beer instead!

Bring a six-pack–actually, bring a case!

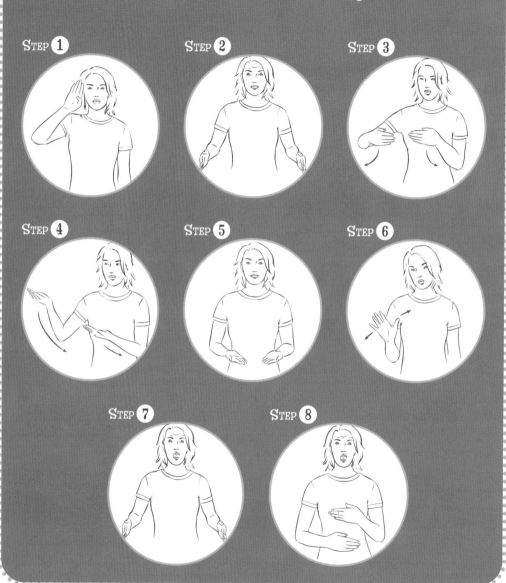

STEP **1**

STEP **2**

STEP **3**

STEP **4**

STEP **5**

STEP **6**

STEP **7**

STEP **8**

Man, you're whipped!

If you're a woman who's easily offended, immediately skip this sign and move on to the next sentence. If, however, you're a woman and want to recognize when your man's friends are ragging on you, then keep reading.

Man, you're whipped!

ASL translation: ([facial expression] + pussy + whip)

 L and A disgusted

 cocked, then straight pursed frown

STEP ❶

STEP ❷ pussy

* Make the most disgusted face you can to show your disdain for your friend's total disregard for the loss of his virility

* Pull down the corners of your mouth

* Furrow your eyebrows

* Place both of your hands in a manual alphabet handshape "L" position and bring them in front of you

* Connect your hands at the thumbs and index fingers

* Bang those handshape "L" signs together twice to indicate a throbbing, powerful, controlling "pussy"

If you were to raise this sign to your chest and place it over your left breast, you'd create the Hearing gesture for "heart," but the Deaf make fun of that because they know the real meaning behind it!

STEP ③ whip

* Cock back your handshape "A" behind your head as if you're holding a bullwhip

STEP ④

* Thrust your cocked handshape "A" forward
* Make a guttural "shi-kaa!" sound to indicate the sound of the bullwhip whipping your pussy friend

What up, dawg?

This sign is a variation on the "What's up?" sign you learned in Chapter 5, with more street attitude.

ASL translation: (event + friend?)

 25 and R

 tilted to the side

 wh-question

 pursed

STEP ❶ event

The "event" or "What's up?" sign is made with handshape "25," and we taught you this sign in Chapter 5 using a matching handshape "25" on each hand. While that's the proper way to sign it, we want to show you here how you'll often see it in the real world—with a single hand that then compresses into another handshape in one movement.

✳ Rest the middle finger of your single handshape "25" on your chest for an instant before you quickly flick your wrist up toward the space near your head....

STEP ❷ friend

✳ Change your handshape "25" into hand-shape "R" by the time it reaches shoulder height

✳ Give that handshape "R" special emphasis with your entire body to indicate the close-ness of your friend and the power of your friendship

✳ Tilt your head a bit to indicate your "wh-question" and your anticipation of an appropriate response from your dawg: woof!

This entire phrase from step one to step two happens quickly and gets thrown around a lot in the Deaf community, so you'll see it often.

Do you think this skirt's too short? Good!

Let's review. So far, we've got you drunk on your ass with a case of beer, we've called out your mother as a lush, and we've successfully insulted your sexual prowess. Now let's find out how you feel about your skirt!

Do you think this skirt's too short? Good!

ASL translation: (skirt-short + really? + good [evil smile])

 Bent B and 1   yes/no question

 sexy tilt   smiling!

STEP ❶ skirt-short

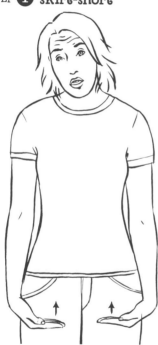

* Making a handshape "Bent B" with each hand, indicate the hemline of your skirt by placing your hands on either side of your thighs

* Quickly move your hands up twice—with a short pause between each move—showing the supershort length of your skirt

STEP ❷ really?

* Make handshape "1" and place your index finger over your mouth as if to say "shush"

STEP ❸

* Move handshape "1" from your lips in a straight line away from your body into the center space in front of you
* Hold that finger there to finish the sign for "really"

> This sign is also used for "true" (but not "truth") and for "sure" (but not "certain").

STEP ❹ good!

The key to getting a knowing, sweet, naughty laugh with this sentence happens here in the final tableau, and it's done without a handshape. Your body language and sexy face bring the fun punch to this sign as you confirm for your listener that, indeed, you love the shortness of your skirt, you knew all along it was too short, and you're leaving it that length to ensure even more fun from your evening out!

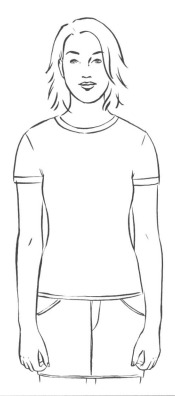

It's girls' night out!

The phrase all men hate to hear is "It's girls' night out!" because it means there'll be lots of late-night-into-morning laughing at their expense, along with tons of fun that will be happening out of range of anything with an XY chromosome pair. Here's how to start your night off right.

ASL translation: (night + women + us-three + go-out)

 Flat B, Bent B, 3, 5, and Flat O   positive

 variable   relaxed

Step ❶ night

Step ❷ women

To sign "girls" in this context, we'll actually sign "women," because the sign for "girl" (created on the side of the jaw) means females who have not yet had their period.

* Make handshape "Flat B"
* Place it palm down with your entire arm bent across your chest—this position represents the horizon of the earth
* Tap twice on the wrist of your handshape "Flat B" with the palm of a handshape "Bent B" to indicate the onset of "night"

* Create handshape "5" and bring the tip of your thumb to your chin
* In a single movement, take that handshape down to midchest and place your handshape "5" thumb tip on your chest

STEP ❸ us-three

In this sentence, we chose to indicate a group of three women by using numerical handshape "3," but your party can be of any number you like—just be sure to use the right numerical handshape to show how many are in your group.

* For our gang of three, create hand-shape "3"
* With knuckles facing outward, horizontally circle that handshape twice fast in front of your body, using your elbow as the rotational axis

STEP ❹ go-out

* Raise your handshape "3" and change it into handshape "5"
* Position that handshape "5" in the same horizontal plane as your head
* Look at your handshape "5" to define location

✳ When handshape "5" is in position near your head, snap it six inches straight out away from your head and, during that movement, close handshape "5" into a handshape "Flat O," to show the world your group has gone out and left behind the whimpering boys!

It's girls' night out!

My husband is driving me crazy!

Janna has never used this phrase about David...to David's knowledge. Though the realism in the facial expression in step two does make him a bit uncomfortable.

ASL translation: (husband + strangle-him)

 Flat B, Bent B, and C

 location specific

 negative

 open-lipped, clenched-tooth fury

STEP ❶ husband

The sign for "husband" is a blending of "male" plus "marry."

* Place one hand in front of your body with palm facing up (that's the "marry" half of the sign)
* Position your other hand flat in front of your forehead
* With your thumb near your forehead, arc that hand (that's the "male" half of the sign) up and away from your face
* Begin to drop that hand down into your waiting handshape "Bent B"
* The instant before your hands touch, that hand becomes a matching handshape "Bent B," so your hands make a quiet clap as they meet each other

STEP ❷ strangle-him

* Your facial expression is wild and angry and your teeth grind
* You become animal-like with raw fury
* Forming handshape "C" with each hand, do the following three things to let the "strangling" begin: indicate the height of your hubby and the size of his neck; tighten your grip; shake until done

Let's put a warm end to this chapter by learning the sign for "family." This is a beautiful sign because it forms the circle of the family in a unifying and intimate way.

 F

 positive (or negative, if you're at odds with your family)

 straight

 straight

STEP **1**

* Create handshape "F" signs with each hand and bring them to the center of your body
* Have each hand lightly touch the other where the index finger and thumb meet on each hand

STEP **2**

* In a fluid motion, twist each handshape "F" hand outward at the wrist so that the outer edges of your pinky fingers touch
* Your "F" handshapes draw an imaginary half-circle in the air during the twist

If you were to raise this handshape position to your eyes, you'd create the universal sign for silly goggles. If you were flicking your handshape "F" signs at each other where they meet, you'd be creating the sign for letting go during a breakup. But we're all about family here, so keep the original handshape "F" in form for now.

It's that smooth movement that gives meaning and coherence to the idea of sewing the family circle. If you were using handshape "U" instead, with the same movement and hand position, you'd be signing "union" (as in "worker's union," not a "married union").

9 Working for the Man

Now let's toss out some signs for the workplace. You can use these excuses conditionally to earn a pass for the day if you sign them clearly, with a dash of earnest and a pinch of pleading.

I'm sorry I'm late.

This classic line is an old chestnut in the office. Learn this sign, use it on your boss the next time you're late, and explain that the reason you're late is because you were learning how to sign this sentence.

ASL translation: (sorry + late)

 A and Flat B

 slightly tilted

 sad

pursed "sorr"

STEP ❶ sorry

* Create handshape "A" and place the palm side on your chest over your heart
* Rub two small circles on your chest

> This sign can also mean "regret" or "didn't mean to."

STEP ❷ late

* Raise your arm and bend it down into an L shape
* Make sure your elbow's in line with your shoulder and, using handshape "Flat B," "paddle" your hand once strongly at the wrist backward about three inches

> The motion of this sign suggests that time has passed by behind you, so don't bend your wrist forward.

Are you sure the clock's right?

If you can't blame yourself for being late to work, blame the clock instead! The secret to making this sign sing is the cockeyed look you'll give to the clock in question. Perhaps with the power of your stare you can force time to move backward.

ASL translation: (time + correct?)

 1 and Flat B

 variable

 yes/no question

 "ti"

STEP **1** time

This is the universal sign for "what time is it?"

* Raise a modified handshape "Flat B" to chest level and then let your hand go limp at the wrist
* With the other hand in handshape "1," tap your index finger twice on top of your handshape "Flat B" wrist
* Look at the clock in question

> Eye direction is vitally important to making this sign clearly. Being precise, even though you're late, is paramount to being understood.

STEP **2** correct

This is also the same as the sign for "right" (as in "correct," not as a direction).

* Create two handshape "1" signs
* Tap one handshape on top of the other one time
* Get your eyebrows up, because you're asking a yes/no question
* Hunch your shoulders and head forward just a bit to indicate that you're anticipating an answer

The train was late.

This sentence is always good for a save if you live near a train because no one can really prove whether you're lying.

ASL translation: (train + delay)

 H and F

 forward

 exhausted

 open "lah" and lots o' tongue!

STEP **1** train

STEP **2** delay

* Using handshape "H" for both hands, make the "H" part of the fingers cross each other in the area in front of your chest, with palms facing down

* Quickly rub the top handshape "H" along the two fingers of the other hand twice

* Use handshape "F" (numerical handshape "9") on both hands and center them close to each other in the space in front of your chest

* Palms face each other and fingers are straight

STEP ③

* "Leap" one hand away from the other in an arcing motion

* Make sure your tongue is hanging out of your mouth to show your exasperation while waiting and waiting for an imaginary train that never showed up

Traffic was horrible.

Another good ruse to use at work is the old stuck-in-traffic routine. Like a delayed train, tight traffic is also hard to disprove, but it's more common in the excuse repertoire, so use this sentence sparingly or it'll wear out your tardy welcome.

ASL translation: (car + traffic)

 Fist and Claw

 forward

 frustrated

 tongue out

STEP **1** car

STEP **2** traffic

* With both hands clenched in a hand-shape "Fist," "grab" the steering wheel of your "car"—hands at 10 and 2

* Turn that steering wheel back and forth as you cruise down the road

* Take two handshape "Claw" hands and bend them both down at the wrists so that the fingertips are pointing at the floor

* Raise your elbows in line with your shoulders

* Place one hand slightly in front of the other

* Stick out your tongue

STEP 3

✳ "March" your hands forward in union a few times down the clogged expressway

Your fingers represent the cars on the street clogging your way. This sign for "traffic" is identical to the sign for "marching"—you can understand why: tight formations, rigid movement forward, and no room for weaving to get ahead through the maddening crowd.

My Kid's sick.

We would never invoke a child to falsely gain favor from an employer, because it sends bad energy out into the world. So let's say, just for energy's sake, that your kid really is ill.

ASL translation: (kid + sick)

 Bullshit and 25

 straight

 negative

 slightly open "si"

Step **1** kid

* Place the index finger of your "Bullshit" handshape horizontally under your nostrils
* The outer edge of your pinky faces away from your body
* Without moving your hand, quickly twist your wrist back and forth ever so slightly an inch each way so that your "Bullshit" handshape jitters like a hyperkinetic kid

Step **2** sick

* Use the trusty handshape "25"— sans quivering middle finger—and stick that middle finger above your eyebrow
* Make your facial expression look as sick as your child
* Think of your handshape "25" finger as a thermometer testing for a fever

The plumber didn't show up.

Specifically blaming other people is an effective way to buy some time if you're late or if you want to head home early from work. A "flooding" house with a plumber who isn't showing up is a quick ticket to excuse paradise.

The plumber didn't show up.

ASL translation: (plumb + person + not-show-up)

 1, V, Flat B, and 5 disappointed

 variable neutral

STEP ❶ plumb

In this first step, you're creating a "pipe" and a "pipe cutter" with your hands.

* Start with the pipe by creating hand-shape "1" in which your finger is the pipe
* Use manual alphabet handshape "V" (numerical handshape "2"/"Scissors" in the "Rock, Paper, Scissors" game)
* Put the "pipe" between your two "cutting" fingers
* Twist your "scissors" back and forth a few times on your pipe finger

This is the sign for "plumb" (ASL translations do not use English endings like "-ing" or "-ed" or "-er").

STEP ❷ person

Okay, now you have to modify "plumb" into a person.

* Center two "Flat B" handshapes opposite each other at shoulder height with palms facing each other
* In a deliberate, single stroke, lower both hands down in a straight line to hip level

That single, straight movement is the ASL modifier for "person" (English "-er") when used in conjunction with a sign like "teach," "work," or "skate."

STEP ③ not-show-up

"Not-show-up" is signed in two steps.

* Begin with one hand in handshape "5" at chest level, palm down
* The other hand is in handshape "1" at a little lower than your handshape "5" near the opposite hip, with finger erect and pointing to the sky

> The handshape "5" is your house and the erect finger in handshape "1" has become the plumber.

STEP ④

* Shake your head in disgust
* Move handshape "1" in an arc underneath your immobile handshape "5"
* Push your handshape "1" finger up through the space between your handshape "5" index finger and middle finger

> Think of handshape "5" as the floor of your house and handshape "1" as the "plumber" popping up (or not!) into your sentence. By shaking your head negatively, you're indicating that the plumber didn't show up. If you had a positive facial expression, you'd be suggesting that your plumber did show up, so, in this case especially, facial expression is the key to understanding the context of the "person" popping up through your floorboards.

I'm gonna throw this computer out the window!

Don't be near a misbehaving computer when you sign this sentence, because the temptation to actually do some tossing out will be too overwhelming!

C, 5, and Flat B   furious!

 follows the flight of the computer   pursed "ca"

STEP ❶ computer

There are many signs for "computer," and they sometimes vary from borough to borough and hood to hood. We'll teach you the most common sign for computer.

* Stretch out a long arm with hand-shape "5" at the end, with the palm facing the ground

* Take your other hand, in handshape "C," and place the bottom of the "C"—the thumb part—lightly on the forearm of your outstretched handshape "5"

STEP ❷

* Slide that handshape "C" up to the bicep of your handshape "5" arm and, the moment it touches the bicep, bring that handshape "C" back down to its original starting position

That traveling handshape "C" suggests the movement of old-time tape reels from giant mainframe computers in days gone by.

STEP ③

Now we need to see your computer. Your computer can be a laptop or a desktop or a Linux server you'll rip from the wall.

∗ Using two handshape "Flat B" hands, grab the sides of your computer and use the space between your palms to indicate its size and weight as you lift it up

STEP ④ throw-out

You've ripped your computer free from its cables!

∗ Your computer is heavy between both handshape "Flat B" hands

∗ Cock the whole thing to your side and tremble under its great weight as you collect the energy to heave it out the window

STEP ⑤

* With every striated muscle fiber in
   your body, fling that computer out
   the window with a "cha!" mouth and
   victory trembling in your fingers!

I'm gonna throw this computer out the window!

STEP **1**

STEP **2**

STEP **3**

STEP **4**

STEP **5**

I'm sorry it's been so long since we've spoken.

This heartfelt statement can go a long way to soothing hurt feelings. The emotion of this sentence is reflected in the graceful movements of your body.

I'm sorry it's been so long since we've spoken.

ASL translation: (long-time + us-two + chat-none + sorry)

 1, K, 5, and Fist   😟 regretful

🙂 straight   👄 blowing air through exposed, clenched teeth

STEP ① long-time

* Begin the apology with handshape "1" on both hands
* Point both index fingers at one shoulder and bend the hands down at the wrists as far as they'll go
* Lift both elbows so you'll have room to make the next movement in front of your body

STEP ②

"Blowing air" as described in Chapter 2 makes an appearance in this "long-time" part of the sentence.

* "Blow air" while moving both hand-shape "1" hands from pointing to your shoulder to pointing straight up to the sky out in front of your body

STEP ❸ us-two

* Place handshape "K" in front of your chest and twist the handshape so that the middle finger is pointing at you

* Bending only at the wrist, alternate moving that handshape back and forth three times in a rocking motion in which the middle finger points at you and then your index finger points at the other person, to indicate "us-two"

STEP ❹ chat-none

* Create identical "5" hands and level them midchest with the palms facing slightly toward each other

* Move each hand outward three inches and then in toward your body three inches in an up-and-down motion three times at a moderate pace

* Your facial expression is especially negative for this part of the sentence

* Shake your head "no" to indicate that you haven't been chatting

> If, however, you had been chatting with your friend, your facial expression would be positive and you'd be nodding your head instead.

> To help you remember this sign for "chat" or "talk," think of one hand as yourself and the other hand as the other person— when your handshape "5" hands move, they're "talking" to each other.

STEP **5** sorry

* With a sad face, create handshape "Fist"
* Make two circles on your chest over your heart to show how "sorry" you are for falling out of touch

I'm sorry it's been so long since we've spoken.

STEP 1

STEP 2

STEP 3

STEP 4

STEP 5

I've been avoiding your calls.

This sentence is blunt, direct, and pulls no emotional punches! It's a dramatic slap in the face.

ASL translation: (you-call-me + avoid-you)

 1, X, and A

straight

 embarrassed

pursed

STEP ❶ you-call-me

Each scrape indicates an incoming "you-call-me" that you will soon be avoiding. Think of the handshape "1" index finger as the telephone line and the scraping "X" index finger as the actual call coming into your phone. (If you reversed the scraping away from your body, you would be the one making all the calls. If you alternated scraping both ways, you'd be making the sign for playing "phone tag.")

* At midchest level, point handshape "1" away from your body
* Take handshape "X" (a bent index finger) and rapidly "scrape" your "X" index fingertip toward yourself along the top of your handshape "1" index finger
* Repeat the "scraping" toward yourself three times

STEP ❷ avoid-you

* Place a handshape "A" at each side in the center space in front of your body
* Both closed hands face in toward each other

One handshape is you. The other is the friend who's been calling you.

STEP ❸

Now it's time to avoid those incoming calls.

* Take the handshape "A" representing you and wiggle it away from the hand representing your friend
* Your eyes must follow the handshape representing you so it's understood that it's you who's doing the avoiding and not your friend

I've been really busy.

Sometimes a look and a single sign are all you need to get your point across, and this sentence is one of those times!

ASL translation: (to-do)

 Q (a.k.a. "The Pincher")   negative

 forward, shoulders hunched   pursed "to"

to-do

You'll use a new handshape for this sentence—the "pinching" handshape (or, if you're following along on your manual alphabet reference page, handshape "Q").

> The pinching suggests "busy," and the movement says you've been "really busy" everywhere with several balls flying in the air.

* Make handshape "Q" by closing both hands into fists and then doing a gentle pinching action with the index finger and thumb of each hand (the pinching does not have to be in rhythm)
* While you're pinching the air, move your arms from right to left
* Cock your head a bit and raise your shoulders

It's lonely at the top.

No one likes a whiner, so when you sign this sentence, sign with arrogance in your eyes and ego flowing off your shoulders like waterfalls.

It's lonely at the top.

ASL translation: (advance + people-look-up)

 Bent B and 5

 variable

 cocky

 pursed

STEP ❶ advance

* Place both hands, in handshape "Bent B," at midchest with the fingertips facing each other
* Your head is cocked to the side
* Your facial expression is anticipatory as you set the starting level for where you were
* Look up, as if you're seeing yourself standing on top of a building

STEP ❷

* Simultaneously lift those two "Bent B" handshapes above your head
* Your eyes follow the movement as you show how far you have risen above the competition

STEP ❸ people-look-up

* Drop your hands and reposition them in handshape "5" in the space in front of your stomach
* Point the fingertips up at yourself
* Keep all your fingers straight, because they represent the adoring crowd looking up at you with admiration

STEP ❹

* Look at the person you're talking to
* Make a cocky face
* Shrug your shoulders as if you don't care whether your peeps love you or not because you're "lonely" and, frankly, lovin' it!

It's good to be king.

Now it's time to claim your royal status. You've earned it!

ASL translation: (rich + look-at-me + king)

 5, Fist, V, and K   regal and self-satisfied

 looking down your nose   pursed "ri"clenched teeth

STEP ❶ rich

❋ Hit your handshape "Fist" into the upward-facing palm of your handshape "5" hand so that it makes a smacking sound

> This sign suggests that you're breaking open a treasure chest filled with the king's riches.

STEP ❷

❋ Position a handshape "5" near your stomach, with the palm facing the sky

❋ Raise your handshape "Fist" up and away from your handshape "5" palm on a diagonal route

❋ While you're moving your handshape "Fist" away, open your fingers into handshape "5" and move each finger individually— they reflect the glinting light of the gold coins spilling from your fist

❋ Your facial expression is smug and satisfied

STEP **3** look-at-me

STEP **4** king

* Make a handshape "V" with each hand and keep both elbows tucked into your sides
* Bend the handshape "V" hands to face you

* To make it clear, however, that we know you are, in fact, a king, and not a court jester or a young prince, take handshape "K" and place it on the opposite shoulder with the palm side in toward your body
* Look down your nose at your minions

Your fingertips are the eyes of the people worshipping you, drooling over you, looking up to you as you address them from the balcony of your castle. Your eyes meet the eyes of your adoring fans; you nod to greet them. Your face expresses that you know you're adored. You know you look good. You know everyone wants to be you.

S<small>TEP</small> 5

* Move your handshape "K" slowly
and elegantly, diagonally across your
body, and land it on your opposite
hip to create your "kingly" sash

It's good to be king! (If you want to be "queen,"
substitute handshape "Q" for the sash; if you
want to be a "prince" or a "princess," substitute
handshape "P" for the sash.)

It's good to be king.

STEP **1**

STEP **2**

STEP **3**

STEP **4**

STEP **5**

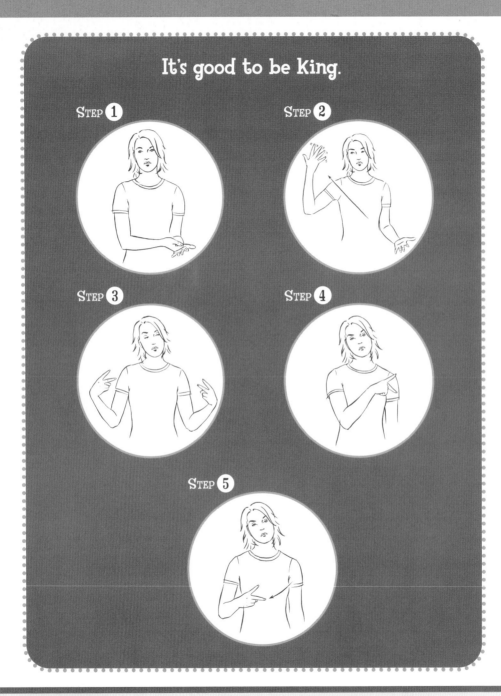

You're fired!

Donald Trump has nothing on you! Strut around the city practicing this sign and you'll be ready to host your own reality show.

ASL translation: (fired)

 Flat B

 straight at the person

 sneering

 curled-lip "fi"

fired

You sign this sentence as if you're chopping off someone's head with an ax.

The slicing "fired" movement should look like a stone skipping across a tranquil lake.

* Place one handshape "Flat B" in front of you, chest high, with your palm facing the ground
* Make a second handshape "Flat B" and face the palm up to the sky
* Take that second handshape "Flat B" and chop the back of it across the top of your other hand

Fist

 serious

straight

 pursed "wo"

* Make a handshape "Fist" with each hand and bring them into the space in front of your torso
* Place one handshape "Fist" over the other and tap the top handshape at the wrist twice against the other wrist

That's the sign for "work" and "job," and it can be used as a verb or a noun. If you've been working really hard, tap your wrists together harder and add some shoulder movement. If you're dreading work, create the sign with normal taps but change your facial expression to "bored to death."

If you were to move both handshapes together in a horizontal circle a few times in front of your body, as if your wrists were invisibly tied together, you'd create the sign for "slave."

10 Health and Emergencies

There are emergencies around us every day, and sometimes getting help in the midst of a crisis can create chaos. This chapter will teach you how to help or to call for help.

Call 911!

Many students believe this urgent request should include the numbers 9, 1, and 1, but it doesn't work that way: 911 is a Hearing term that was invented for voiced communication over the telephone, so 911 doesn't have the same ring of authenticity for an emergency in Deaf culture. When an emergency arises in the Deaf community, there are many ways to get help. Some call 911, hoping their TTY call will be answered. Some call 711, because they know a relay operator will answer the line with a TTY. Others use pagers and the Internet to get the word out. This sign tells someone to get help immediately—the person receiving the sign will decide how to get that help.

ASL translation: (contact-to + emergency)

 25 and E

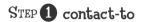 straight

 urgent

 pursed "e"

STEP ❶ contact-to

* Make both hands into handshape "25"
* Bring one hand up to shoulder level and twist it in at the wrist
* Angle the other handshape "25" across your chest and make that palm face the other palm
* Raise your eyebrows and tap your middle fingers together twice to create the sign for "contact-to"

STEP ❷ emergency

* Raise handshape "E" to shoulder level, twist the palm outward, and arc it back and forth across your body six inches in each direction
* Your facial expression is wide-eyed, with eyebrows up and mouth open

Do you need a doctor?

You usually see this sign constructed using a letter "D" for "doctor," but that's an awfully English and Hearing way to create this sentence.

ASL translation: (doctor + need?)

 Flat B and X

 straight

 yes/no question

 lips open, pronouncing "nee"

STEP ❶ doctor

* Make two handshape "Flat B" hands
* Hold one up at shoulder height with the edge of your palm facing outward
* Tap the fingertips of your other hand against the heel of the first hand two times, with eyebrows raised and mouth slightly open

You're taking the pulse of a patient in this sign. As we said earlier, you might see this signed with a manual alphabet "D" for "doctor," or "N" for "nurse," but both of those signs, using the first English letter of the name, are more PSE than ASL.

STEP ❷ need

* Make handshape "X" in the space in front of your chest
* Quickly dip that hand downward twice, like a fishing line bobbing on the water, to indicate "need"
* Your facial expression is questioning
* Your shoulders are forward
* Your head is tilted forward
* Your eyebrows are up

I'm not feeling well.

Here's a good sign that's quick to learn, and which can also mean "sick," "ill," or "blah."

ASL translation: (sick)

 25

 tilted to the side

 droopy

pursed "si"

* Raise handshape "25" and press the middle finger against the side of your forehead, as if you're checking for a fever
* Your facial expression matches how horrible you feel
* Droop your eyelids
* Turn down the corners of your mouth
* Look like death itself, and if you're mistaken for a corpse, you'll know you made good with this sentence

I hurt my _____.

Sometimes you're so hurt you can't speak. This next sequence of fill-in-the-blank sentences will help you communicate your pain. The setup for each sign is identical. Only the specific place that hurts will change.

I hurt my _____.

To make these signs to indicate pain, you can use two hands, one hand, or no hands. A "no-handed" pain indicator is done with your eyes, head, and whole body. This can be hard to make clear at first if you aren't experienced, but you can practice: look at your elbow, then look at the person you're trying to tell that you have pain in your elbow, then look again at your elbow and make your facial expression reflect pain while your entire body "reacts" in pain the instant you look at your sore elbow. That's whole-body communication and pure ASL without using your hands.

ASL translation: (pain-here)

 1

straight

 negative!

variable

arm

* Use handshape "1" with one hand to indicate the area of pain
* "Throb" your "1" up and down to indicate the electrical pulses in your arm that are creating the stinging pain
* Your facial expression is pained

head

If you bonk your head...

* Use two handshape "1" signs to locate the pain and throb at the specific location
* Wince as you simultaneously throb your fingers

The smaller the throb space between your fingers, the more precise the area of pain.

belly

If you have stomach pain...

* Take two handshape "1" hands and frame the source of the pain between your two index fingers
* Throb the index fingertips at each other, with the pain in between them
* Twist your wrists as you rhythmically throb your fingers
* Hunch your shoulders
* Raise your eyebrows
* Your facial expression is anguished

leg

Two handshape "1" signs on the leg can indicate a larger area of pain.

* Run your "throbbing" index fingers up and down your thigh from hip to knee
* Your facial expression is exhausted from the pain

That wide swatch indicates a generalized pain rather than one that's localized to any specific place.

Do you prescribe medicinal marijuana?

We don't want to encourage the breaking of any laws, so we're going the legal "medicinal marijuana" route here, but that doesn't mean the unscrupulous among us can't ask this same question—using an ironic facial expression to flip its meaning in another direction—on the street to a person who may or may not be dealing legally...with life.

Flat B, 25, F, and Flat O

 yes/no question

 straight

 relaxed "med"

STEP ❶ medicine

* Raise one handshape "Flat B" to midchest with the palm facing the sky
* Place the middle finger of a handshape "25" on the other hand in the center of your handshape "Flat B"
* Press that middle finger into your palm, anchor it there, and rock that handshape "25" gently back and forth three times without lifting it from your palm

STEP ❷ pot

* Bring a handshape "F" to the corner of your mouth to create the universal sign for toking a doobie!
* Move that handshape toward and away from the corner of your mouth a few times
* Your facial expression is as high as a kite!

This sign indicates "medicine"—you're re-creating the old mortar and pestle, in which your middle finger is the pestle and your hand is the mortar and the thing being crushed between your finger and palm is the medicine.

STEP **3** give

The question mark in an English sentence is always performed as a yes/no question facial expression in ASL. If you were giving someone a prescription for medicinal marijuana, your facial expression would be positive and decisive. The difference between deciding and asking can be overlooked in ASL, so make sure your facial expression is always strong one way or the other.

✳ Bring your hand down from beside your face and make a handshape "Flat O" (flatten out a regular manual alphabet "O" handshape just a bit) in front of your torso

✳ Center the edge of your palm in handshape "Flat O" against your stomach and then move it away from your body in a small six-inch arc that indicates "give" or "prescribe"

✳ Raise your eyebrows, open your eyes, and hunch your shoulders forward to indicate that you're asking a question

Where's the bathroom? I think I'm going to puke!

If you've been drinking too much and toking up isn't settling your stomach, you may find the emergency need to hurl. This sentence will earn you the porcelain throne faster than all the gold in all the land.

Where's the bathroom? I think I'm going to puke!

ASL translation: (bathroom + where? + feel + throw-up)

 T, 1, 25, and 5   wh-question

 varies   pursed "vom"

STEP ❶ bathroom

* Make a manual alphabet handshape "T" (poke the thumb up between a handshape "Fist" index finger and middle finger of the same hand)
* Shake that "T" back and forth sideways a couple of inches a few times in a swift and deliberate manner
* Your facial expression is distressed

STEP ❷ where

* Shake handshape "1" at the wrist (with the back of your hand facing you)
* Your facial expression is desperately inquisitive, with eyebrows down

This "T" represents the toilet, and while it's very English to use the first letter of the word as its name sign, that's the way it is in ASL when it comes to signing "bathroom," "toilet," or "potty."

Step ❸ feel

* Place the middle finger of a handshape "25" in the center of your stomach
* Move it up your body a few inches
* Thrust it out and away from the center of your body in an arc so that it ends a few inches away in the space in front of your chest

Step ❹ throw-up

Here's a recap of the fantastic "throw up" sign that you learned in Chapter 7.

* Open your mouth and place handshape "25" near the bottom of your mouth with the thumb pointing at your chin
* Thrust that handshape away from your mouth in a large arc, landing it in the space in front of you

Fire can bring warmth and light or it can burn you to death. We'll teach you the negative form of fire here with a facial expression that is fearful and alert, with sharp movements. If you were to suggest a warm and comfy fire in a fireplace, your facial expression would be positive and joyful. This sign for fire is not the same as the sign for "setting a fire" or the "getting fired" from a job sign that you learned in Chapter 9.

 A and 5
straight

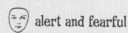 alert and fearful
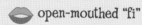 open-mouthed "fi"

STEP **1**

* Make two "A" handshapes in front of you with your palms facing up
* Give your hands some heft by pretending a wooden log is balanced across both hands

STEP **2**

* "Burst" your "A" hands into two "5" handshapes
* Wiggle your fingers back and forth on each hand as you deliberately raise your hands up to frame your face
* Your facial expression is frightened and open-mouthed

Your fingers indicate the flickering flames of the fire.

11 Hooking Up

This is the chapter you've been waiting for! These pick-up signs will enliven your dating life and win you bar bets if you play the signs right.

Check that badonkadunk/baby got back!

There's no better compliment a man can pay a woman than to comment on her ass. If you believe that, keep reading, and develop this sentence into a serious statement of truth. If, however, you're just looking for some fun and innocent joshing, then add a little funky attitude. This sign is suggested in the movement of your handshapes and for that reason is both elegant and obscene. Watch and learn!

ASL translation: (middle-figure [narrow] + lower-figure [wide])

 Flat B and Claw

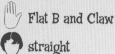 straight

 cha!

 cha!

STEP 1

* Raise two "Flat B" handshapes to shoulder height
* Palms face each other
* Keep your elbows tucked into your sides
* Move your handshapes down and in, to form the classic V shape of a woman's torso

STEP 2

* When you reach the bottom of the V, explode both "Flat B" hands into dual "Claws" while mouthing "cha!"

You're creating the dimensions of the badonkadunk you're describing. If that butt is meaty and juicy, squeeze your "Claw" hands a bit to indicate the delights waiting for your good lovin'.

I wanna get with you.

You'll see as we move along in this chapter that these sexual signs are extremely visual and graphic. In many ways, this chapter is perfect for advancing your ASL skills. This sentence is blunt, so let's get on with it.

I wanna get with you.

ASL translation: (get laid-with)

 Fist and H

 straight

 flirty

 flat and firm

STEP **1**

* Center two "Fist" handshapes in front of your body with the palms facing the sky
* Tuck your elbows into your sides
* Flex your arms to create tension in your fists

STEP **2**

* Both of your handshape "Fist" hands jump into handshape "H" position
* Raise the index and middle fingers together on each hand by flicking them up from your fists

The two fingers on each hand represent two bodies about to get it on. You're one body, and the person you wanna get with is the other.

＊ Now twist your handshape "H" bodies up, around, and "into bed" by simultaneously turning each handshape in toward the center of your body

You'll know you're performing this part of the sign correctly if those fingertips create a perfect circle in the air as they move from step two to the final position in this step.

Was that a Kiss, or were you trying to eat my face?

If you find yourself wetted in places you did not expect—and did not enjoy!—this little sentence will dry you off fast.

ASL translation: (that + kiss + lick + bite + which?)

 Y, Flat O, H, Claw, and A wh-question

 straight puckered

STEP ❶ that

* Raise a handshape "Y" from the manual alphabet near your face and then drop it down in front of your body
* Stop when it reaches the area in front of your stomach

This is the sign for "that," which sets up the context and definition of the "that" in the signs to come.

STEP ❷ Kiss

* Create a handshape "Flat O" and use the tips of that hand to "kiss" the side of your face

You might even move your head to the side a bit to indicate the strength of the kiss pressed into your flesh.

STEP ❸ lick

* Transform your handshape "Flat O" into a handshape "H"
* "Lick" your handshape "H" "tongue" up and down the side of your cheek in the grossest possible way
* Your facial expression should reflect the negative effect the licking is having on you

STEP ❹ bite

Here's the "bite" of this sentence.

* Change your handshape "H" into a handshape "Claw"
* "Chomp" at the side of your face where you were previously kissing
* Open your mouth a bit and tilt your head away from your chewing hand

STEP **5** which

* Your facial expression is in wh-question form
* Both of your hands are in "A" handshapes
* Raise your thumbs and point them to the sky as if giving the thumbs-up sign
* With your head cocked, your eyebrows down, and your shoulders hunched forward, wait for a response as you move your hands up and down in opposite directions a few inches each way

The reason each handshape "A" moves in a different direction is because you're giving your listener a visual clue that you're asking for a choice between two separate things. If your hands were moving in unison, you'd be suggesting you were lifting something instead of seeking an answer to your question: kiss, lick, or bite?

Was that a Kiss, or were you trying to eat my face?

STEP

I like beer.

Let's head to the bar and sign up a storm to express your thirst for beer. You're not wildly in love with beer—you have a platonic relationship with the heady brew on a strictly "friends" level.

ASL translation: (beer + like)

 B, 25, and 8

 straight

 positive

 pursed "b"

STEP **1** beer

You learned the sign for beer in Chapter 8, but since the facial expression is different here, we're illustrating it for you again.

* Create handshape "B" in which your thumb is positioned over the palm
* Place the index-finger side of the handshape next to your cheek
* Make two quick strokes down your face three inches or so
* Your facial expression is excited—express your like for beer with eyebrows up and anticipation in your eyes

STEP **2** like

* Position handshape "25" in front of you with the palm facing your chest
* "Pluck" at your chest with your middle finger and thumb (creating numerical handshape "8" in the process)

> You've picked your like from inside your body and made it externally known.

I prefer wine.

Your feelings about wine are incrementally stronger than they are about beer, so let's set up that preference.

ASL translation: (wine + prefer)

 W and 25

 straight

 satisfied and strong

 pursed "wi"

STEP **1** wine

STEP **2** prefer

* Position your handshape "W" next to your cheek
* Make two small circles with your palm toward your face

The two circles might remind you of swishing a bit of wine in a glass before giving it the thumbs-up or thumbs-down.

* Take handshape "25" and tap your chin twice with the tip of that middle finger
* Your palm is facing your body and the fingers and thumb of the "25" hand-shape are spread out
* Your facial expression is serious

I love whiskey!

You are a whiskey hound! Use this sign with the right attitude and you're certain to win a shot or two on the house.

ASL translation: (whiskey + love!)

 Bullshit and Fist   serious Love

 straight   pursed "wh"

STEP ❶ whiskey

* Make the "Bullshit" handshape on both hands
* Place them in front of the center of your body
* Your elbows are close to your sides
* With palms facing in opposite directions, tap the bottom edge of one hand against the top edge of the other, twice
* This sign for "whiskey" is the same as the sign for "liquor," so you should purse your lips into a "wh" position

STEP ❷ love

The kind of love you're expressing here is crazy—it has nothing to do with the physical or the heartfelt. This love sign is used to indicate the "most-best-ever," and you can use it in many different circumstances.

* Make a handshape "Fist" and bring the back of your hand to your lips as you actually kiss the back of your hand loud enough to make a sound
* Then strongly pull the handshape "Fist" straight away from your mouth to put the exclamation point on the love

LIKE, PREFER & LOVE

You've learned three great modifiers with "like," "prefer," and "love," and you can use them to set up quick sentences with other words you've already learned. For example, "I love monsters!" (monster + love) or "I prefer badonkadunks" (badonkadunk + prefer). Mix and match words and see what fun you can create on your own.

like

prefer

love

Let's do shots.

This sentence takes several ASL sign concepts and compresses them to communicate its essence.

ASL translation: (come-on + drink-it)

 Bent B and Single C

 straight

 challenging and inviting

 slightly open, pronouncing "co"

STEP **1** come-on

* Use your handshape "Bent B" to cast a "come-on-over" invite to your friends
* Open your mouth a bit and cock your head to make the "come" command clear

STEP **2** drink-it

* Modify your handshape "C" sign to make it into a "Single C" handshape by having only your index finger and thumb create the "C" shape while the rest of your fingers are curled into your palm. This "Single C" represents your fingers wrapped around a shot glass.
* Pick up that shot glass from the bar, slam the shot down, and then quickly bring the "Single C" up to your lips and throw it back
* If you're feeling it, wipe your lips with the back of your hand

Your place or mine?

They're closing down the bar and throwing you out. You're desperate. You're looking for a little fun to finish the night. Go make an offer you hope cannot be refused.

ASL translation: (your + home + fuck + my + home + doesn't-matter)

 Flat B, Flat O, Fist, and 5   yes/no question

 varies   pursed "fu"

STEP **1** your

* Make a handshape "Flat B" with your palm facing the person you're talking to and then push that handshape straight out at them a few inches

STEP **2** home

* Make a handshape "Flat O" for "home" by touching the tips of your fingers against the side of your chin and then moving the handshape to your cheekbone
* Your facial expression and your eyebrows are neutral

STEP ❸ fuck

In the Hearing world, this sentence can be flirty and abstract and coy. In the Deaf world, however, there can be no doubt about the intent: "Let's get down to fucking!"

* Change your facial expression to sneering
* Use "Fist" handshapes and place one "Fist" over the other in front of your body with the palms facing each other and your elbows cocked away from your body
* Press the upper "Fist" down into the space above the other fist in a humping, pumping motion

> This sign is the hardcore Deaf way to sign the kind of "fuck" you're talking about in this specific sentence. Using this "fuck" in the right context will win you admiration in the Deaf community for knowing such insider slang signs.

STEP ❹ my

Now that the "fucking" part of your proposition is over, switch your tone to offer your home for the getting down.

* Place a handshape "Flat B" palm on your chest to indicate that you're welcoming your new friend to do the dirty deed at your joint

Step ❺ home

Step ❻ doesn't-matter

Finish the sentence with
"doesn't matter."

* Create handshape "Flat O" to make the sign
  for "home" again by touching the tips of your
  fingers against the side of your chin and
  moving the handshape to your cheekbone
* Your eyebrows are up to ask a question
* Your facial expression is expectant as you
  await a response to your offer

> While this sign is identical in movement
> to step two, it's the facial expression
> that's important here.

* Use the yes/no question facial expression
  to indicate that you don't care either way
* Your handshape "5" hands are held in
  front of your chest with the palms facing
  you
* Then move your hands back and forth a
  few times in opposite directions
* The tips of your fingers touch and bump
  into each other as they pass

Your place or mine?

Choice Word   SEXY/HOT/LUSCIOUS!

This universal sign is a ton of fun and means "sexy" and "hot" and "luscious."

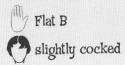 Flat B

slightly cocked

 flirty

luscious "se"

* Move both handshape "Flat B" hands in unison as you exaggerate the outline of a beautiful woman's body: round breasts, thin waist, perfect ass
* Move your arms sensually and lustfully to get your point across
* Look at the shape you're creating and enjoy it!
* Lick your lips!
* If you're describing a guy with fabulous muscled arms, six-pack abs, and a tight butt, make your handshape "Flat B" motions reflect the hardbody you're "seeing"

The key to this sign is to enjoy it and to "feel" the curves and muscles of the body you're creating out of thin air.

I just moved you to the top of my "to do" list.

A compliment can go a long way. This sentence in the Hearing world may be couched and flirty, but, again, in Deaf culture this sentence means one thing and one thing only: "You're next on my list for fucking!"

Bent B, Flat B, G, 1, Flat O, and X   cunning and sexy

 varies   pursed

STEP **1** list

* Form handshape "Flat B" into a piece of paper positioned near your head, with the palm facing your other handshape "Bent B"

* Place the "Bent B" at the top of your "Flat B" and then lift and replace it again and again on your palm to indicate your long list

STEP **2** to-do

* Keep your handshape "Flat B" list and change your handshape "Bent B" into a handshape "G"

* Pinch and then release your handshape "G" index finger and thumb together three times, indicating "to-do," as you move that hand in a circle

STEP ❸ you

* Change your handshape "G" into handshape "1" and point at the person, indicating the "you" you're going to move

* Handshape "Flat B" remains in its original step one position

STEP ❹ bottom-to-top

* Keep handshape "Flat B" and make your handshape "1" hand into handshape "Flat O"

* "Move" the name of the person from the bottom of the list and place it from "bottom-to-top"

* Do that by "picking up" the name with your handshape "Flat O" fingertips from the palm of your handshape "Flat B" and "depositing" the name at the top of your "list" on the fingers of your handshape "Flat B"

✳ Drop your handshape "Flat B" list and change your handshape "Flat O" into a handshape "X"

✳ Touch the edge of that "X" to the side of your face near your eye, then lift it off your face and immediately replace it on your chin to say "sex," so there's no doubt about what you mean by moving your friend to the top of your "to-do" list

I've moved you to the top of my "to do" list.

STEP **1**

STEP **2**

STEP **3**

STEP **4**

STEP **5**

Screw me if I'm wrong, but haven't we met before?

We conclude this chapter, and this book, with the world's cheesiest pick-up line. Enjoy!

ASL translation: (before + intercourse?)

 Flat B, O, and 1

 straight, bent forward

 yes/no question, eyebrows up

 pursed "be"

STEP ① before

* Handshape "Flat B" stands straight and is parallel with the front of your body
* Fingertips are facing the sky
* Bend your fingers as if pushing air over your shoulder

> That motion of putting something behind you is the sign for "before."

STEP ② intercourse

* Make handshape "O" at your hipline
* Handshape "1" hovers near your upper chest
* Your facial expression anticipates an answer to this yes/no question—your eyebrows are up, your head is cocked forward
* Insert your handshape "1" two inches into the center of your handshape "O," and then pull it out a little and stick it back in and pull it out a little

Congratulations!

You've just finished learning some ASL concepts in the sort of chatty and informal teaching style we like to use with our students. We don't curse (much) in class, but we wanted to give you an insider's glimpse into the real world of the Deaf community. Sometimes cussing and crassness and being politically incorrect are part of it. We hope you've enjoyed this brief journey into ASL and Deaf culture. There's a lot left to learn, but you now have a great grounding in the reality of how the Deaf communicate with each other every day. It was our great honor to serve up this *Hand Jive* for your consumption.

How David Met Janna

We're often asked how we met and why we got together because, after reading everything so far, it seems unlikely a Deaf woman from Iowa and a Hearing man from Nebraska would get along (and we're not just talking about state football rivalries here), let alone stay married for more than eighteen years. We have lived many of the challenging issues between the Deaf and the Hearing, and we've laughed and cried over them all. Here's how the story began....

To understand Janna, we have to go way back to when she was born. Janna has an older brother and sister who are ten and eight years older, respectively. Her mother, father, sister, and brother are all Hearing. Janna was born Deaf because of an RH factor conflict—a blood incompatibility between her father's and mother's blood types. RH factor incompatibilities can be deadly, and they are very tricky because they don't necessarily become a problem in the first pregnancy or two. That's why, in years gone by, people were required to get blood tests before they married to make sure their blood was "compatible" in the event they wanted to have children. If the baby's blood type is different from the mother's, there can be problems, but modern medicine can work around that now without a threat to baby or mother, and in many states blood tests are no longer required as a prerequisite for marriage.

Janna was born in 1963 during the start of the Rubella epidemic (1963–1965). Rubella is a respiratory virus that, if caught while pregnant, can cause Deafness and physical deformities in babies. Twenty percent of "Rubella babies" die within the first year of life.

Janna was born into the "Golden Age of the Deaf" with thousands of other children, and even though her Deafness was caused by a blood-type incompatibility and not Rubella, she benefited from all the new services created for those Deaf children. Entire Deaf institutions were created to handle this influx of Deaf infants into the social system.

For the first five years of her life, she did not speak. Janna was born without a language, and, because her parents were Hearing and she was exposed to no sign language over those five years, technically her first "native" language is actually English, even though she was born into the culture of the Deaf. American Sign Language is Janna's second language, according to linguistic anthropologists. Interestingly enough, ASL was accepted as her "foreign language" requirement at City University of New York's Lehman College after she petitioned the dean's office to have ASL officially accepted as her second language because, at that time, American Sign Language was not considered a foreign language at Lehman College.

Janna's parents did not know she was Deaf. It was Janna's kindergarten teacher who discovered that Janna did not hear. On the first day of class, when roll was called, Janna did not respond to her name. That teacher, in a mainstream Hearing school, said, "There's something wrong with Janna," and had her hearing tested. When Janna was tested and it was discovered that she was Deaf, she was enrolled in the Iowa School for the Deaf, where she was able to communicate, blend in with her peers, and advance her education on a fast track.

When Janna's mother was asked why no one in the family knew there was something wrong with Janna's hearing for the first five years of her life, she said, "We thought it was strange how close she sat to the television with her ear pressed against the speaker, but we just thought she was stupid." That blunt answer was pretty common back in the 1960s because, until the Rubella outbreak forced the breaking of new research ground in infant Deafness, not a lot was known in the general population about Deafness or the Deaf community. Out of the tragedy of not knowing, or of not wanting to know, came positive changes for the Deaf that are still resounding today. Janna is fond of saying that her kindergarten teacher saved her life, while the Iowa School for the Deaf saved her mind.

David met Janna during a play contest in North Platte, Nebraska. Both had just graduated from college, and Janna was starring as Sarah in the play *Children of a Lesser God*, and David had written and directed an original play. The moment David saw Janna, he was in love and knew he wanted to be with her forever.

On the cusp of saying good-bye after the play contest, a classic Nebraska blizzard blew in and socked in both show casts. David, seeing the snow as a sign of his forever wish being granted, hunted down Janna, and for three wintry days they communicated by writing back and forth on Holiday Inn stationery. Janna was uncertain if mixing Deaf and Hearing cultures would work in the long run, but David was persistent in his belief that everything would be fine, and they would last at least eighteen years together.

The courtship was fast and deep. Janna made it clear that she would not use her voice and that ASL must be the shared language. David agreed and purchased a TTY so he could directly communicate with Janna. Janna taught him ASL, and, eighteen years later, David is still learning new signs and concepts; the learning curve only gets higher and harder the longer you study ASL.

Together they piled into a car and moved to Washington, D.C., where they lived for a year and participated in the Gallaudet march on the Capitol. A year later, they were married in New York City, and the rest of the story is in this book.

RESOURCES

Staying in touch with Janna and David

You will always find the latest updates and corrections to *Hand Jive* by visiting us online at **http://HardcoreASL.com**. You may also email us by writing to **touch@HardcoreASL.com** and we'll get right back to you.

You can also watch videos we made starring Janna that demonstrate many of the phrases in the book at **http://HardcoreASL.com/handjive/**

David's *Urban Semiotic* blog has a section that deals with Deaf issues and *Hand Jive*: **http://UrbanSemiotic.com/category/deaf/**

Books

A Journey into the Deaf World, by Harlan Lane

A Place of Their Own: Creating the Deaf Community in America, by John Vickrey Van Cleve and Barry Crouch

The American Sign Language Dictionary, by Elaine Costello

The American Sign Language Phrase Book, by Lou Fant

The Autobiography of Helen Keller, by Helen Keller

The Book of Sign Names, by Samuel J. Supalla

Forbidden Signs, by Douglas C. Baynton

Grammar, Gesture, and Meaning in American Sign Language, by Scott K. Liddell

Linguistics of American Sign Language, by Clayton Valli and Ceil Lucas

The Mask of Benevolence, by Harlan Lane

Sign Language Among North American Indians, by Garrick Mallery

The Week the World Heard Gallaudet, by Jack R. Gannon

When the Mind Hears, by Harlan Lane

Movies

Black
Mr. Holland's Opus

Plays

Children of a Lesser God (also a movie, but the play is better)
The Miracle Worker (also a movie, but the play is better)

Websites

American Sign Language Browser: **http://commtechlab.msu.edu/sites/aslweb**
Gallaudet University: **http://www.gallaudet.edu**
Iowa School for the Deaf: **http://www.iadeaf.k12.ia.us**
League for the Hard of Hearing: **http://www.lhh.org**
National Technical Institute for the Deaf: **http://www.ntid.rit.edu**
National Theatre of the Deaf: **http://www.ntd.org/index.html**

Index of Words and Phrases

Index